Thinking Strategically in Turbulent Times

An Inside View of Strategy Making

Foreword by Barry Z. Posner

Alan M. Glassman,
Deone Zell, and Shari Duron

M.E.Sharpe
Armonk, New York
London, England

Library of Congress Cataloging-in-Publication Data

Glassman, Alan M.
 Thinking strategically in turbulent times : an inside view of strategy making /
by Alan M. Glassman, Deone Zell, and Shari Duron.
    p. cm.
 Includes bibliographical references and index.
 ISBN 0-7656-1251-8 (cloth : alk. paper) — ISBN 0-7656-1252-6 (pbk. : alk. paper)
  1. Strategic planning. 2. Business planning. 3. Hewlett-Packard Company—Planning.
4. Los Angeles County (Calif.)—Politics and government. 5. California State University—
Planning. I. Zell, Deone. II. Duron, Shari, 1945– III. Title.

 HD30.28.G58 2005
 658.4'012—dc22   2005007421

Printed in the United States of America

| BM (c) | 10 | 9 | 8 | 7 | 6 | 5 | 4 | 3 | 2 | 1 |
| BM (p) | 10 | 9 | 8 | 7 | 6 | 5 | 4 | 3 | 2 | 1 |

Contents

Foreword

This is a powerful book. Powerful not only for what it finds, but also powerful for what it does not find. Based upon extensive interviews with key informants, the authors report that the strategic planning process (and substance) is different across the private, public, and not-for-profit sectors (Hewlett-Packard vs. Los Angeles County vs. the California State University system). And, in the end, they also find that the process is largely driven by similar trends and pressures across the sectors and serve more common than different aspirations.

These are great stories. While those people familiar with any of these particular organizations or the broader settings and environments in which they reside will know that the situations have changed somewhat since these stories were collected, this does not diminish the power of the first-person narrative and voices of those directly involved in the strategic decision processes. Indeed, these snapshots only reinforce the complex and dynamic processes involved and give proof to the somewhat cynical comment: "If anyone tells you that they are not confused about what's going on these days, you can be sure that they don't have the first clue."

One striking conclusion from this report is that strategy formulation is a messy political operation and that the planning process, too often considered as the end objective, is but a means to better strategic execution. What we find in these stories is evidence for how strategic planning provided a mechanism for reconciling, at least for a moment, disparate perspectives, juggling competing priorities, and influencing competing constituencies. The "plan"—however recorded and memorialized—served not so much as providing street signs and numbers on houses as it did the names of major towns and cities along the way to some place we had never been before. An important outcome was agreement, not necessarily on the particulars, but on the big picture and an overall commitment throughout these large-scale organizations to some key values and principles. They roughly pointed people in the same direction, without herding them all down the same narrow road.

I was particularly struck by the largely positive and optimistic nature of the senior leadership of these vast enterprises (some of the giants of their species, say the authors). Even while acknowledging the political and economic turbulence, marketplace uncertainty, relentless pace of technological change, escalating competitive pressures, and the like, these leaders spoke with a can-do and will-do attitude about meeting these realities. And, they were realistic; there was no kidding around about the challenges, but the voices were strong, and mostly healthy, in expressing the sea captain's viewpoint that "there are always storms at sea; we've weathered them before and we'll weather them again."

Indeed, one of the great strengths of this book is that we get an inside view of the strategic thinking processes of these three organizations, as well as a look inside the head of dozens of senior executives. *What* are they thinking and *how* are they thinking about the meta-challenges they (personally and organizationally) are facing? The analysis provides a deeper appreciation of the collective and political processes required to build the coalitions and consensus necessary to get everyone on the same page and heading in roughly the same direction. It confirms my belief that we must hear the voices of leaders to gain a deeper appreciation of the skills needed to navigate complex organizational environments.

We're going through another round of strategic planning in my organization right now. This is probably true for your organization too. And, if not, it only means that you are in the white space between the current and the future plan and responsible for executing against the current plan, while anticipating the future one. I feel and experience exactly what Alan, Deone, and Shari heard from their informants: "Here we go again; when will this ever be finished?" "There's so much work to be done and where am I going to find the time, and energy, for this?" "Everything is changing so much around here, why bother to spend all this time planning?" "Can't we start this next year?" "Things seem to be mostly working; why do we need to make any changes?" "My part of the organization is fine, let them work on the parts that aren't doing well."

But, such moans have little impact, and the process continues. And, in the process, I come to be re-energized with a better sense of both purpose and direction. I come to realize that my particular concerns are shared by other parts of the organization, and that our challenges, across my part of the enterprise, are not so dissimilar from the ones within any part of the organization. I see creativity and imagination that are literally forced by the process of confronting realities that previously were ignored or kept out of sight. Lots of people, up and down the hierarchy, are talking with one another about their aspirations for the future rather than complaining about the ubiquitous "they" and "them" in charge of this place. And, I remember that, as so often is the case, the journey is the destination.

Barry Z. Posner
Dean and Professor of Leadership
Leavey School of Business
Santa Clara University

Preface

Across sectors, as organizations entered the twenty-first century, leaders attested to a bewildering pace of change in their external environments and acknowledged the significance of strategy making and strategy execution to their overall organizational success. As noted by many observers and practitioners of the strategic planning field, the latter included such common themes as imprinting an inspired vision on the organization, conducting detailed environmental scans, identifying strategic issues and appropriate strategies, and aligning resources and support systems during implementation. Yet, as leaders have became more sophisticated in the "mechanics" of the strategy-making and strategy-execution processes, we have also heard increasing discontent, characterized by such statements as "We spent months and months developing our strategic plan only to see it relegated to a shelf to gather dust" and "No sooner had we developed our strategic plan than a major, unexpected event occurred in our external environment that rendered our effort moot." For those of us interested in applied research, we wondered about the inner dimensions of the leadership experience as they searched for new and better ways to help their organizations adapt to increasingly turbulent environments.

This book represents the culmination of a sustained effort to understand the underpinnings of strategy making and strategy execution as seen through the eyes of organizational leaders, an in-depth undertaking that began in 1999–2000. At that time, recognizing that we were fortunate to have access to three premier organizations representing a fascinating cross-section of the economy —Hewlett-Packard, Los Angeles County, the California State University— we investigated (through interviews) each system's use of information technology (IT) as an "enabler" for strategic planning. Our findings presented at a "showcase session" of the Academy of Management in Washington, D.C., in 2001 generated discussion well beyond our IT focus, as many of our colleagues persistently sought to learn more about the internal aspects of these three strategic planning processes. Subsequently our enthusiasm intensified as we realized that the use of technology represented a window of opportunity into the inner workings of how these three giants were adapting to their environments. So we launched a formal study of their environments and the use of strategic management as an adaptive tool, as described by key senior managers.

Armed with an interview guide, tape recorders, and notepads, we approached our initial interviews with some trepidation, wondering if our interviewees would share candidly their personal feelings about "coping" with the pace of environmental change and their honest assessment of their organizations' strategy-making and strategy-execution processes. In return for assurances that we would provide them a chance to review their quotes for accuracy, they granted us permission to use their real names to lend authenticity to the study. It is noteworthy that only a few edits occurred during the review, such as the removal of an explicative or an embarrassing reference to another individual. Mostly, except for some grammatical smoothing, the quotes remain unaltered. The result is the following book, which presents our findings through "executive voices."

The book can be used at several levels: (1) as a classroom companion to help students grasp the impact of the pace of change on organizations and their leaders, as well as the current difficulties associated with strategy making and strategy execution in these turbulent times; (2) as a bridge for scholarly comparative studies of different sectors; and (3) as another exemplar for reinforcing the importance and richness of applied qualitative studies for understanding organizations. We hope you find the words of these leaders and our interpretation of sector similarities and differences informative.

Acknowledgments

As colleagues, we learned much from each other during this journey. From Shari's knowledge on the inner workings of a global organization and the possible lessons for other sectors to Alan's thirty years of organizational change and strategic planning consultation with senior managers across sectors to Deone's expertise in organizing and understanding large qualitative data bases, our personal perspectives expanded greatly.

We would like to thank the leaders at Hewlett-Packard, Los Angeles County, and the California State University—our three giants—who participated in this study and, importantly, waived anonymity to provide authenticity and additional context. We are particularly grateful to the following individuals who quickly expressed support for the project and helped us identify and recruit the participants: Susan Cook and Mike Northcott from H-P; David Janssen and Sharon Harper from Los Angeles County; and Charlie Reed and Sandra George from the CSU. In addition, we thank Richard West, Jon Fullinwider, Soren Kaplan, Gerry Rossy, and Wayne Smith for early explorations on the topic of enabling technologies and strategic alignment, which evolved into this larger study.

We also wish to thank several individuals who have encouraged us throughout our careers through thought-provoking conversations and wise counsel: Tom Backer, Kim Boal, André Delbecq, Bob Hanna, Anne Huff, Kurt Motamedi, and Buzz Wilms.

We are most appreciative of the technical support provided by the Management and Organization Development Center, School of Business Administration at California State University, Northridge, particularly the oversight and coordination by Elizabeth Barrett and the exacting and diligent editing by Rana El Ghadban. Lastly, thank you Harry Briggs, our editor at M.E. Sharpe, who, based on a brief presentation at a Western Academy of Management meeting, recognized the possibility of a book and "nudged" us to pursue this study.

Thinking
Strategically
in
Turbulent Times

— 1 —

Introduction:
The Contextual Framework

Think in anticipation, today for tomorrow, and indeed,
for many days. The greatest providence is to
have forethought for what comes.
—Baltasar Gracian, Spanish Jesuit

It is the last lesson of modern science, that the highest
simplicity of structure is produced, not by few elements,
but by the highest complexity.
—Ralph Waldo Emerson
Goethe; or, the Writer (1850)

It has become commonplace to describe today's organizational environment as messy, frenzied, disordered, and even chaotic. At the simplest level, observers attribute this condition to the increasing pace of change, often citing advances ranging from new applications for robotics and laser technologies to the emergence of nanotechnologies to the potential benefits of quantum computers and genetic engineering. Indeed, there is near unanimity that the world has entered an era of unparalleled turbulence, reflecting the entwined forces of technological, biotechnological, and communication advances. It is not unusual for managers to note the vagaries and increased competition of a new global marketplace along with the unrelenting demands by customers for improved quality accompanied by their limited loyalty to their service and product providers. Yet other observers and practitioners note the challenges of recruiting, developing, and managing the new workforce, characterized by greater diversity in ethnicity, age, and education, and exacerbated by worker demands for new experiences and increased responsibility.

3

Still others highlight the ongoing redesign of organizations to be more responsive to their environments, the management of knowledge, and the importance of continuous reinvention and transformational leadership. As projected by Senge et al. (1999:3):   *link to Jane*

> Look ahead twenty or thirty years. Does anyone expect the next twenty years to be less tumultuous than the last twenty years? Given the changes expected in technology, biology, medicine, social values, demography, the environment and international relations, what kind of world might humanity face? No one can say for sure, but one thing is reasonably certain: Continuing challenges will tax our collective abilities to deal with them. Failure to rethink our enterprises will leave us little relief from our current predicaments.

Equally important, as put forth by Mazmanian (2004:1), the impact is far-reaching:

> The dynamic forces of technological innovation, market orientation, increased mobility, global competition, deregulation, and changing public expectations and needs are affecting every major aspect of the economic, political, and social spheres of society. This is profoundly challenging those in business, government, and civic society to adapt or be relegated to the sideline of history. There are winners and losers emerging from the transformation between old- and new-age businesses, innovative and traditional governments, between works within and across industries, between different regions of the nation and around the globe, between professions and those with different skill sets, and between those with the talents and aptitude to succeed in the more rapidly changing world of information and technology than the more stable arrangement of the past age.

Operating in such an environment tends to be emotionally and physically taxing, akin to Vaill's (1989:ch. 1) observation that we have entered a world of "permanent white water," where the old operational rules are inadequate and leaders are asked to take on greater responsibility for what is less and less controllable. As asserted by Lissack and Roos in *The Next Common Sense* (2000:inside flap), organizational environments have shifted from being complicated to being complex:

> The old common sense was about how to deal with the separate and free-standing units of a *complicated* world. The next common sense is about mastering the *complex* swirl of interweaving events and situations around us. . . . The new world is a complex one of arrows rather than boxes, of interactions rather than entities.

Figure 1.1

Organizational Environments

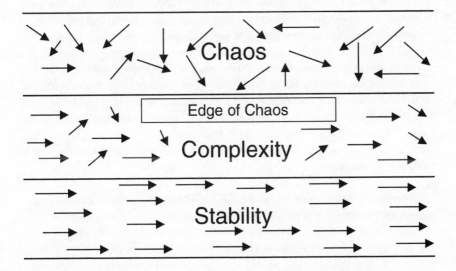

It is argued that today's leaders must abandon organizational designs and accompanying processes based on the Newtonian concept of an orderly, predictable universe that assumes an understanding of each component leads to an explanation of the whole; rather, leaders must embrace the emergent complexity sciences and accept the notion of nonlinear systems where subtle, perhaps unobservable, events can dramatically impact their organizations (c.f., Stacy et al., 2002; Marion, 1999; Brown and Eisenhardt, 1998; Wheatley, 1992). It negates the view that stability is a primary metric for organizational excellence (Stacy, 1992:43–44).

We have adopted the phrase *turbulent times* to capture both the increasing pace of change and the uncertainty or dynamics of organizational environments.[1] As shown in Figure 1.1, turbulence (as demonstrated by the arrows) occurs in two worlds: (1) Chaos, where we intellectually know that order exists, but we also understand that we cannot discern that orderly state within the organizational environment, and (2) Complexity, bounded by stability on one side and chaos on the other, where overall directional order is identifiable, but the organization continually experiences unexpected "lightning bolts" from or "stochastic shocks" within the environment. As explained by an executive friend from the consumer products industry:

It seems that nearly every day I receive surprising information about a competitor's new or improved product, or a distributor's logistical problems, or a major customer's unhappiness with our service, or even a legal action that requires my involvement—it is very, very difficult to stay focused on our strategic initiatives. . . . I have simply accepted that I live with continuous uncertainty; I live on the edge of chaos . . . and that my job is to make sure that others do not lose sight of the ends we seek.

From our perspective, this statement describes the world where today's leaders must increasingly make their strategic choices. And, as noted by Weick (2001:153), "stochastic environments represent a moving target for learning because they can change faster than people can accumulate knowledge about them. When recurrence is scarce, so is learning." ⋇

Defining Turbulence

Environmental turbulence, as defined by academe, is an extension of environmental uncertainty, which is typically defined by two factors:

1. *Environmental complexity:* This refers to the number, strength, and dissimilarity of external forces or pressures (e.g., competitive actions, technological advances, economic conditions) affecting an organization (Child, 1972). The greater the number and heterogeneity of these forces, the more complex the environment and, consequently, the more difficult to predict and control.
2. *Dynamism:* This refers to (a) the predictability with which the aforementioned forces are changing and (b) the actual rate of change of the forces (Miller and Friesen, 1983). A dynamic environment occurs when the forces shift quickly and/or abruptly with little or no warning (Jurkovich, 1974; Dess and Beard, 1984; Duncan, 1972).

The more complex and dynamic an organization's environment, the more uncertain it becomes. When multiple forces in an organization's environment change simultaneously, the environment is said to be turbulent (Daft, 1998; McCann and Selsky, 1984). We need to note, however, that individuals can experience the same environment differentially. As summarized by Hatch (1997:89), "The same environment might be perceived as certain by one set of managers and uncertain by another . . . environments do not feel uncertain, people do." In fact, McCann and Selsky (1984:461) assert that only when the environmental conditions make an individual's continued adaptation survival uncertain, can the label turbulent be truly applied. And, as

McCann and Selsky also note (1984:460), sometimes the environment becomes hyperturbulent, that is, the environmental forces are beyond the adaptive capacity of the organization's management.

Therefore, to understand strategy making in turbulent times, it is necessary to understand the individual perspective on the environment. If Einstein believed that time is relative to the entities experiencing it, would it not be the same for turbulence?

A Cross-Sector Phenomenon

Since the publication of books such as *Managing in Turbulent Times* (Drucker, 1993), *Hypercompetition* (D'Aveni, 1994), *Blur* (Myer and Davis, 1998), and *Competing on the Edge: Strategy as Structured Chaos* (Brown and Eisenhardt, 1998), there has been a tendency to attribute this era of turbulence primarily to the private sector, particularly high-technology organizations. Such a conclusion would be wrong! In the public sector, for instance, Peters and Savoie (2001:3, 6–7) foresee a disordered future for government:

> The signs of real change . . . are everywhere . . . there are too many variables, too many forces at play, and too many unknowns for either scholars or practitioners to feel sure about what the future may hold for the civil service. . . . The policy environment is marked by great turbulence, uncertainty, and an accelerated pace of change.

Similarly, Kiel (1994:9) contends that the intersect between shrinking public budgets and citizen demands for both better services and accountability has turned government into "nonlinear, complex systems filled with change and flux," while Glassman and Winograd (2004:329) declare that under the rubric of reinventing government, public-sector leaders are exploring "leadership strategies to transform their units into adaptive agencies that are able to adjust to an increasingly tumultuous environment." As suggested by Mazmanian (2004:2), "It is requiring establishment of new forms of policymaking, policy implementation, and compelling a rethinking of how best to apply public authority."

Equally turbulent environments have also emerged in the social and higher education sectors. Assessing the challenges confronted by nonprofit leaders, Nanus and Dobbs (1999:11–16) highlight eleven major concerns, including items such as adapting to frequent changes in statutory requirements, designing more responsive and efficient infrastructures through the use of information technology, meeting a new set of health and security demands (e.g., care for an increasing number of uninsured poor, basic shelter and food requirements for an aging population) and shifting priorities among philanthropic foundations and other donors. And, while it is easy to argue that the social sector is distinctive, the authors' conclusion sounds very similar to the turbulence described by their private- and public-sector brethren (1999:48–49):

> In light of these changes and the uncertainty they engender, it is not surprising that the leaders of nonprofit organizations are experiencing a great deal of turbulence and confusion. Conflicting forces and pressures are pulling and pushing their organizations in every direction. They know that they can no longer get by with business as usual, and they are constantly being challenged to find new, more effective ways to deliver services. At the same time, they're well aware that the need for services is growing while the human and financial resources they need for performing those services are not keeping pace.

In the same way that observers have seemingly underrepresented the turbulence in the nonprofit sector, we hear little about the supposedly staid world of higher education. Yet, in recent years, America's system of higher education has had to absorb/respond to a set of formidable, interrelated demands (RAND, 1996, 1997, 1998; Brand, 1994; Taylor et al., 1993): (1) economic resources expended on higher education have declined steadily as other societal demands competed successfully for federal and state funds and as budget deficits resulted in a fundamental shift in municipal priorities; (2) technology advances have raised questions concerning both the appropriateness of traditional pedagogical approaches and the financing of new equipment and the accompanying investments in ongoing faculty development; and (3) broad-based demographic shifts have increased the tension over the meaning of diversity in higher education, propelling campuses to the forefront of the dialogue on cultural identity, the meaning of assimilation, and social justice. As summarized by the Association of Governing Boards of Universities and Colleges (1992:8), in this environment "institutions of higher education that do not rethink their roles, responsibilities, and structures . . . can expect a very difficult time. . . . Some will not survive." Concurring, Zemsky (1995:12) asserts that we must totally redo higher education to be more responsive to the emergent dynamic environment, noting that while current efforts at "retrenchment, reorganization, restructuring, and reallocation activities have helped institutions . . . they are not in themselves transformative."

In summary, then, at the beginning of the twenty-first century, all sectors of our society have experienced increased environmental uncertainty that requires rethinking organizational designs and processes. In very similar statements, observers and practitioners highlight the impact of technology on operational efficiency and competitiveness, demands for better services and/ or products, and shifting demographics. In all sectors there are survival worries and an understanding that "business" needs to be done differently.

The Strategic Process and Turbulence

For most of the past three decades, organizations have followed a predictable and established approach to strategic planning, using it as a mechanism for: (1) rigorously assessing the organization's internal and external environments, (2) debating and determining mission, values, and goals, and (3) developing an appropriate yet flexible set of operational strategies and objectives. Often referred to as the *deliberative approach* to strategy making, it emphasizes rational thought and step-by-step consensus decision making, and the belief that once implemented, the strategic plan, as articulated at the outset, can be realized as originally intended (Hax and Majluf, 1996:17–18). It is a tightly controlled, learnable process (Mintzberg et al., 1998:28–33). It is also the approach taught in business schools throughout the United States.

Strategic planning is controversial, however, because the outcomes of the deliberate formulation process often fail to materialize during implementation. As summarized by Keller (1997:ix) whose assessment of higher education reflects anecdotal findings in the other sectors:

> In the past dozen years, hundreds of the 3,500 colleges and universities in the United States have launched efforts at strategic planning. . . . A few institutions have transformed themselves dramatically . . . many institutions have stumbled, dissolved into controversy, or lost their nerve. Exactly why some have succeeded while others have floundered is not clear. Few scholars have studied the many attempts at strategic change in higher education.

Simply stated, Hamel (1996:70) says that "strategic planning isn't strategic any longer," arguing that we must revolutionize strategy formulation from a ritualistic, reductionist, extrapolative approach to a more inquisitive, expansive, inventive approach. At root, the problem appears to reflect the historic and prescriptive separation between formulation usually conducted at the executive level and implementation by ill-prepared line employees (c.f., Gray, 1986:89), (or) thinking and acting (c.f., Pfeffer & Sutton, 2000:ch. 1; Mintzberg, 1994b:273–274), (or) event-driven and outcome-driven efforts (c.f., Weick, 2000; Mintzberg, 1994b:83–87). With increasing frequency, however, the traditional approach is simply viewed as too cumbersome for today's fast-paced environment (Cusumano and Markides, 2001).[2] According to Eisenhardt (1990:39):

Strategy making has changed. The carefully conducted industry analysis or the broad-ranging strategic plan is no longer a guarantee of success. The premium now is on moving fast and keeping pace. More than ever before, the best strategies are irrelevant if they take too long to formulate. Rather, especially where technical and competitive changes are rapid, fast decision-making is essential.

Day (1999:48) presents a somewhat visceral description of the line manager's response to implementing conventional strategic planning in a turbulent environment:

> By the mid 1980s, top-down strategic planning was in disarray; line managers either tolerated it or dismissed it as irrelevant, strategic actions couldn't be implemented, and the intrusions of strategic planning were widely resented. Many companies enthusiastically dismantled their planning groups. What happened? 1) the necessary conditions of stability that made a command approach feasible were out of step with the turbulence most businesses were facing; 2) the fuel for strategic planning is valid and timely information, but in fast moving markets the filtered information . . . may be obsolete or biased before it can be fed into a top-down decision process; 3) companies found that the simplistic prescriptions of the planning tools . . . were often misleading or wrong.

As stated by Collis and Montgomery (1995:118), "the armies of planners have all but disappeared, swept away by the turbulence of the past decade."[3] In recognition of this ongoing predicament and today's increasingly turbulent external environment for most organizations, both academics and practitioners have proposed a shift from conventional strategic planning to strategic management, which occurs on a continual rather than periodic basis and becomes the shared responsibility of the entire organization rather than a practice reserved for senior management (Hunger and Wheelen, 2001:3–5). Referred to as the *emergent approach* to strategy making, it assumes that few organizations can realize their intended strategy and that strategy can be understood only from the patterns or consistencies observed in past behavior—where a realized pattern was not intended (Hax and Majluf, 1996:17; Mintzberg et al., 1998:189–201). Accompanying this awareness is the growing realization that the agility to lead an emergent strategy-making process is created not through the use of standardized procedures or *recipes*, but through carefully facilitated and purposeful social interactions that accelerate the creation and diffusion of strategic idea making (c.f., Meyer, 2001; Faulkner and Campbell, 2002:9; Sullivan, 1998; Eisenhardt, 1990). As put forth by Khatri and Ng (2000), "strategic decision making has to take into account both rational and intuitive processes." More specifically, in this environment, the strategy-making process must be accelerated to achieve what Meyer (2001) refers to as "second generation speed" as differentiated from first generation speed that focused on speeding up and streamlining operations using such techniques as business process engineering. Contrasting the two worlds of strategic planning, D'Aveni (1994:237) states:

> Current views of strategy are inadequate to deal with the competitive environment. . . . The formal approaches to strategic planning are more appropriate for environments of traditional, slower and less aggressive competition . . . these environments are characterized by long periods of stability between disruptions. These periods call for more emphasis on carefully considered thought and deliberate action. Hypercompetitive environments, on the other hand, draw more upon the *instant reaction and reflexes* of the company. It is the difference between the rigidly planned and carefully orchestrated invasion, as practiced by the German military in World War I and World War II, and attacks based on the doctrine of flexible response, as practiced by the U.S. military in the 1990s. Strategy in the current environment is more a process of fine-tuning reflexes and searching out or creating temporary opportunities than it is a product of long and deliberate planning of specific actions in product markets.

Thus the current era of turbulence alters the focus of strategy making from a deterministic process to a search for coherence among innumerable variables. Cusumano and Markides (2001:4) postulate that it is the shift from science to art:

> The common *belief* is that it is possible for a company to design a superior strategy; and it is possible for others to learn the art of crafting superior strategies—it is an art. It is the art of asking intelligent questions, exploring possible answers, experimenting with possible solutions, and starting the thinking process all over again by questioning the answers arrived at a year or two before. Effective strategic thinking is a process of continuously asking questions and thinking through the issues in a creative way. Hence, correctly formulating the question is more important than finding a "solution." Thinking through an issue from a variety of angles is often more productive than collecting and analyzing unlimited data. And actually experimenting with new ideas is often more critical than scientific analysis and discussion.

Similarly, Mintzberg (1994b:331–332) and Brown and Eisenhardt (1998:236–239) emphasize the need to synthesize soft data and continually introduce innovation and creativity into the strategy-making process. For instance, we are aware that more and more organizations, regardless of sector, are using versions of scenario planning to "unfreeze intellect, allowing intelligent people a framework within which it is . . . mandatory to admit that they do not know what the future will bring" (Ringland, 1998:190). Scenarios augment strategy by considering possibilities rather than the probabilities associated with conventional strategic planning.

The Leadership Connection

Senior managers, in all sectors, frequently convey that their most important responsibility is to think strategically about the future direction of the organization, process new and discontinuous information, and then make appropriate decisions. But, as asserted by Mintzberg (1994a:110), "Where in the planning literature is there a shred of evidence that anyone has bothered to find out how managers make strategies?" Moreover, as noted by Albano (2002:1), "The ways of thinking that underlie strategy formulation are seldom addressed in business textbooks." Similarly, in a recent assessment of the culminating strategic planning course found in most MBA programs, Greiner et al. (2003:402) "contend that . . . schools have moved away from interdisciplinary thinking and practice toward an almost exclusive emphasis on theory and analysis." The authors grieve the loss of experiential learning where students debated possibilities and learned to integrate different perspectives.

Our own review of cross-sectorial books on both strategic planning and leadership indicate that few details exist to describe how managers actually (1) think about the increasing pace of change and their specific environment, (2) think about their organization's strategic planning process, and (3) think about their personal approach to strategy making. Rather, the emphasis has shifted to rules and guidelines on how leaders can create an "adaptive culture where behavior is flexible" and "managers initiate change when needed, even if it involves risk" (Daft, 1998:338). The goal is to have enough latitude to remain as close to equilibrium as possible. Within this framing, some see an analogy with the improvisational behavior often found in music and the theatre arts. Commenting on the similarities between the legendary band The Grateful Dead and the world of managers, Brown and Eisenhardt (1997:32) state:

> For the band, the challenge is how to create a fresh musical experience with changing musicians and audiences, while doing so at a particular time, with a limited repertoire, within a limited amount of space and budget, in concert after concert. . . . For managers, the challenge is very similar: to

master both adaptive innovation and consistent execution . . . again and again and again . . . in the context of relentless change.

The authors note that this requires constant awareness of each other; ongoing, often subtle, communication; and a set of clearly understandable and specific rules (Brown and Eisenhardt, 1997:33). Likewise, in a study of 12 firms in the computer industry, Eisenhardt et al. (1997:3) found that "The most effective decision makers relied on limited structure in their strategic decision processes," while Moorman and Miner (1998) suggest that improvisation can improve organizational learning and memory by generating experiments and fostering the emergence of higher level competency. While we are drawn to these constructs, we are also aware that a significant void still exists regarding how senior managers actually steer their organizations in turbulent times. We are intrigued by the broad question: In turbulent times, how do you define the leadership mind vis-à-vis strategy making?

The Three Giants' Study

This book reports on a qualitative study of the strategic planning experience of senior managers at three giant organizations, representing three different sectors: Hewlett-Packard, a Fortune 50 company; Los Angeles County, the largest municipal government in the United States; and the California State University system, the largest public higher education system in the world. While diverse in their missions, all three were experiencing profound changes in their external environments at the time of the study and senior managers had experienced the limitations of the traditional approaches to strategic planning: they were searching instead for techniques that were (1) better integrated with day-to-day operations and (2) better suited to a turbulent, fast-paced environment. Table 1.1 provides basic information on each.

The overall objective of the research was to determine how senior managers approached strategy making in environments characterized by speed and uncertainty. The main sets of research questions were:

1. How do senior managers characterize their environment in terms of both the pace of change and strategic issues? What are the sources of environmental uncertainty and disorder?
2. How do senior managers approach the strategy-making process? What specific roles do senior managers play in the strategy-making process? Can we ascertain the thought processes used by senior managers to determine strategies?

Table 1.1

Organizations Studied

Sector	Hewlett-Packard Private	County of Los Angeles Government	California State University Higher Education
Number of Employees	140,000	89,000	40,000
Organizational Structure	4 business units	38 departments	23 campuses

3. Can the characteristics of an emergent model of strategy making be identified?

Methods

Qualitative methods were chosen due to the study's exploratory nature and to enable the topics under study to be investigated in depth and detail. In particular, the study followed the principles of "grounded theory"—essentially a set of methods that, when followed, ensure that themes and relationships between them are generated inductively through close contact with the empirical world (e.g., "grounded" in the data), rather than logically deducted from a priori assumptions. The grounded theory approach advocates for example, that (1) researchers remain objective by suspending preexisting biases and beliefs; (2) individuals and/or organizations be "theoretically sampled" for inclusion in the study based on their contribution to the development of theory; (3) the use of coding procedures to build from the concrete to the abstract; and (4) iterative analysis of data using the *constant comparative* method in which emerging themes are repeatedly compared to existing data to ensure that they are valid[4] (Glaser and Strauss, 1967).

Sample

Between November 2002 and February 2003, interviews were conducted with a total of 43 senior managers at the three organizations.[5] We sought to interview senior managers from as wide a range of functional units as possible (in the case of H-P and LAC) and from as many and as diverse campuses as possible (in the case of the CSU) to access the greatest diversity of viewpoints and opinions (see Table 1.2).

Table 1.2

Interview Sample

Hewlett-Packard	Los Angeles County	California State University
Executive Vice President (1)	Chief Administrative Officer (1)	Chancellor (1)
Senior Vice Presidents (5)	Assistant Chief Administrative Officer (1)	Executive Vice Chancellors (2)
• Office of Strategy & Technology	Auditor-Controller (1)	• Academic Affairs
• Printing Group	Department Heads (9)	• Administration & Finance
• Research and Development	• Fire	Presidents (11)
• Enterprise Marketing Group	• Human Resources	• Chico
• Corporate Affairs	• Internal Services	• Fresno
Vice Presidents (5)	• Mental Health	• Fullerton
• Storage Group	• Parks and Recreation	• Los Angeles
• Strategy & Business Development	• Probation	• Northridge
• Strategic Change and Integration	• Public Works	• Pomona
• Mobile Solutions	• Senior and Community Services	• San Francisco
• Supply Chain	• Sheriff's Department	• San Jose
Directors (2)		• San Luis Obispo
• Enterprise Group		• San Marcos
• H-P Services		• Sonoma
Internal Strategy Consultants (4)		

Data Collection and Analysis

Interviews were semistructured and open-ended, permitting flexibility in asking follow-up questions and enabling interviewees to provide in-depth responses in their own words. Through this approach, we could both ask a standard set of questions and pursue probing or clarifying questions as they came to mind during the interview process. Allowing respondents to answer in an open-ended fashion made it possible to view the world of change and strategy making through the respondents' eyes, or get "inside" their heads to understand the issues and themes from their points of view. It also made it possible for respondents to provide additional data that did not follow directly from the interview questions, which they believed were critical to understanding their perspectives.

In most cases, interviews were conducted by all three authors to enable comparative data analysis later on. All interviews were tape-recorded with the permission of the interviewees. Interviews lasted approximately 1–1½ hours each, and focused on two main areas: (1) the organization's environment; and (2) the strategy process. The methodology and interview protocol are contained in Appendices A and B.

All interviews were transcribed, entered into a computer database, and analyzed using a software package for qualitative data reduction and analysis called NVIVO (available from QRS International).[6] Following accepted procedures for qualitative data analysis, a set of codes then was developed to enable the sorting of exemplars (chunks of text) into categories (Miles and Huberman, 1994). Codes were based both on the research questions and on themes and issues that emerged during the process of data analysis (see Codebook in Appendix C). For example, codes were developed to represent the organization, the interviewee, the forces that emerged, perceptions of the environment, the strategic planning process, and a variety of themes related to it (e.g., the role of leadership, lessons learned, etc.) Using NVIVO, the fieldnotes and exemplars that represented the codes were then electronically "tagged" for later retrieval.[7] Data analysis was then conducted by iteratively "cross-tabulating" various codes. For example, cross-tabulating the forces that emerged by the organization provided a list of forces experienced by each organization. Further cross-tabulating these results by individual made it possible to determine the number of individuals from each organization who had identified any given force. The cross-tabulating procedure also produced quotes that were used in writing the findings. During the coding process and before writing the results, emerging findings were discussed and debated at length by the three authors, to help ensure that the results were not swayed by any one researcher's preexisting biases and beliefs.

Appendix A. Detailed Methodology

In this appendix we further discuss how our research methods and the use of NVIVO, a software program for qualitative data reduction and analysis, enabled the development of grounded theory in this study. As discussed earlier in this chapter, grounded theory advocates that:

- Researchers remain objective by suspending preexisting biases and beliefs.
- Individuals are theoretically sampled for inclusion in the study based on their contribution to the development of theory.
- Coding procedures are used to build from the concrete to the abstract.
- Data are analyzed iteratively using the constant comparative method in which themes are repeatedly compared to existing data to ensure they are valid.

Remaining Objective by Suspending Preexisting Biases and Beliefs

The first step in building theory from the ground up was to recognize the potential existence of preexisting biases and beliefs on the part of the authors, which may have accumulated through years of experience or outside influence (e.g., reading and conversations with others). For example, all three authors had read much literature (e.g., books and journal articles) that professed that the pace of change is fastest in the high-tech sector and slowest in government and higher education. Another potential preconceived belief was that speeding up the strategy process would require doing away with many elements of the formal, rational approach. We attempted to identify and "suspend" these preconceived notions by holding regular, in-depth conversations in which we questioned and challenged each others' assumptions, and in many cases played the "devil's advocate." Once such assumptions were articulated, they could be systematically debunked, making it possible for us to avoid reading them into the data.

The avoidance of preconceived biases and beliefs was further encouraged through the use of rigorous and detailed coding procedures designed to build conclusions inductively from the ground up rather than deductively from the top down.

Theoretical Sampling of Subjects for the Development of Theory

Rather than select a random sample, as is typically done in quantitative, experimental studies, individuals in our sample were selectively chosen based on their ability to contribute toward the development of "theory"—for example, patterns and relationships regarding environmental turbulence, emerging models of strategy making, and the relationship between them. Our criteria for selecting individuals to interview were as follows: they (1) were in top-level positions; (2) had broad knowledge of the organization's environment; and (3) had knowledge of, or were directly involved in, the organization's strategy process. Refer to Table 1.2 for the resulting sample.

Use of Coding Procedures to Build from the Concrete to the Abstract

Grounded theory is developed by building inductively from the concrete to the abstract, or from detailed facts to general principles. This principle was accomplished primarily through the use of the NVIVO software package for qualitative data analysis and reduction. The first step was to create a codebook that represented both preexisting and emergent themes. Preexisting codes were those that we had in mind before data analysis began—for example, those that represent the research questions, such as "strategy process." Emergent codes were those that arose during the process of data analysis, such as "terrorism" or "customer demands." In NVIVO, the creation of preexisting codes is accomplished through the use of "tree" nodes, named because they can be structured hierarchically. The "tree" can have multiple levels or branches of nodes to represent a nested, or branching structure. The creation of emergent codes is accomplished through the use of "free" nodes, which do not assume a hierarchical structure and are used for the temporary storage of emergent themes and ideas.

The emergent data process is enabled by NVIVO's ability to create, move, merge, or delete nodes as data analysis proceeds. At any point in time, for example, a code can be created and stored as a free node that can later be turned into a tree node by cutting and pasting. All data represented by the free node are automatically incorporated into a tree node. Similarly, the contents of any tree node can be easily moved, for example from one branch of the tree to another, simply by dragging or cutting and pasting the icon from one branch to another. The content automatically follows. The same process can be used to merge two nodes into one, or to delete an entire code. For example, if one is confident that data will surface to substantiate a node, one may establish a code (either free or tree) at the outset. Over time, however, as the coding process unfolds it may become clear that the code is not sufficiently substantiated—for instance because only one person talked about it. In this case the code and the accompanying text can simply be left out of the analysis or deleted from the database.

The following example may help make this process clear. In identifying the nodes representing the environmental forces, our goal was to come up with relatively mutually exclusive codes (e.g., "technology" and "housing costs"). Often, however, the distinction between codes was not clear, or there was an obvious relationship between them. For example, our initial coding scheme considered the codes "competition," "focus on cost," and "commoditization" to be separate and distinct. However, through the process of repeatedly applying them to chunks of data, over time it became clear that they were so interrelated that they belonged together in one code. Closer analysis enabled us to hypothesize that a causal relationship existed between them (for example, intense competition brought about the focus on cost, which was dealt with through commoditization). One indication of such interrelationships was that in coding the data, the same chunk of text received multiple codes (e.g., focus on cost and commoditization) because the interviewee talked about them in the same sentence, or breath. Or in other cases, even though individuals discussed them distinctly, their cause-and-effect relationship was so clear that it was obvious that the data should be subsumed under one code. Another example was the codes "globalization" and "connectedness." In determining whether these should exist as separate or identical forces, it was necessary to analyze the relationship between them. For example, was connectedness a result of globalization, or the cause? And so on.

Another aspect of NVIVO, the availability of document *attributes,* enabled comparisons between the three different organizations. In essence each document, or fieldnote, can be assigned any number of attributes, which can be thought of as "demographics" (e.g., the name or type of the organization, or the individual him- or herself). These attributes can then be used to "cross-tabulate" the data. For example, to explore the differences in competition between the three organizations, one asks the software to cross-tabulate the "competition" node by the "organization" attribute, producing a 2 × 3 matrix. Each cell of the matrix contains all the text pulled up by the requested combinations of nodes. One then reads the text to discern patterns in the data. For example, this cross-tabulation revealed that competition is a far greater threat at H-P than at either LAC or the CSU.

The iterative, emergent nature of grounded theory was further enabled by the use of *memos* in NVIVO. Essentially, as one reads through the fieldnotes, one can record electronically mental notes or interpretive thoughts through the use of memos. These memos themselves represent text, or data. They can thus be re-entered back into the database and coded using the codebook, just like the raw fieldnotes. (Raw data are distinguished from memos by using different names for the codes. To formalize the distinction, one could use the attribute feature and assign corresponding attributes to the two.) This process ensures that emerging interpretations are never lost, and can be used to build on each other.

In sum, the various features of NVIVO enabled us to develop themes in an iterative, emergent nature, and to build "theory"—or patterns and relationships between variables or groups of variables—inductively from the ground up.

Iterative Analysis of Data Using the Constant Comparative Method

NVIVO also enables the use of the constant comparative method, which requires that themes be repeatedly compared to existing data to ensure that the themes are valid. Specifically, as the codes are applied, they are consistently compared to the text being used to substantiate them—and as a result are either refined, moved, merged, deleted, and so on. The more data that accumulate under a code, the more substantiated or "mutually exclusive" they become and the more clearly relationships between codes (e.g., between commoditization, competition, and focus on cost—as well as between globalization, geopolitical issues, terrorism, and corporate scandals) can be discerned.

The ability to cross-tabulate codes by organization, using the attribute function, helps to further substantiate themes by providing further insights into the relationships between codes. For example, while in one organization three codes—commoditization, competition, and focus on cost—may "hang together" and therefore be discussed together (as was the case at H-P), at another organization such interrelationships may not exist or are not apparent. This was the case in the CSU, where the relationship between competition and focus on cost was far less apparent. These two codes were therefore considered mutually exclusive, and discussed separately.

Appendix B. Interview Protocol

Background

- What is your position?
- How long have you been in this position?
- How long have you been with your organization?

The Environment

- What major environmental forces [e.g., technological, political, demographic] have you witnessed in the last few years, and how have they affected your organization?

- How do these compare to what was affecting your organization in the past?
- How would you describe the environment in which your organization operates? (Probe: In terms of pace of change? Predictability? Chaos? Turbulence? And so on.)
- Has the environment changed, relative to the past (e.g., 5 or more years ago)?

Strategy Process

- Please describe your organization's strategic planning process.
- Has your organization's strategic planning process changed significantly in the last few years? If so, how, and why?
- What are your personal thoughts about the strategic planning process— for example, how effective it is? Do you believe in it?
- Have your views toward strategic planning changed at all? What "lessons" have you learned?

Appendix C. Codebook

1. Organization
   - (1)   Hewlett-Packard
   - (2)   Los Angeles County
   - (3)   California State University
2. Individual
   - (1)   (list of 43 individuals)
3. Environmental Forces
   - (1)   Focus on cost
   - (2)   Technology
   - (3)   Terrorism
   - (4)   Commoditization
   - (5)   Demographics
   - (6)   Legislative
   - (7)   Board
   - (8)   Customer demands
   - (9)   Housing costs
   - (10)   Merger
   - (11)   Union
   - (12)   Globalization
   - (13)   Genomics
   - (14)   Connectedness
   - (15)   Labor costs

   (16) Economy and budget
   (17) Employee turnover
   (18) Media
   (19) Staffing needs
   (20) Political pressure
   (21) Accountability
   (22) Competition
   (23) Immigration
   (24) Uncertainty
   (25) Culture
   (26) Organizational form
   (27) Training
   (28) Corporate scandals
   (29) Accountability
   (30) Health crisis
  4. Perceived pace of change
  5. Strategy
   (1) Process
   (2) Historical perspective
   (3) Themes and issues
     1 Alignment
     2 Attitudes toward
     3 Barriers to
     4 Centralized vs. decentralized
     5 Communication of
     6 Cross-sector comparison
     7 Formal vs. informal
     8 Future of
     9 Implementation
     10 In turbulent environment
     11 Leadership in
     12 Lessons learned
     13 Link with budget
     14 Longevity
     15 Metrics
     16 Participative
     17 Role of technology
     18 Tools and techniques
     19 Variations on strategy

— 2 —

Thinking Strategically at Hewlett-Packard

To decades of business students and entrepreneurs, Hewlett-Packard has served as a metaphor for the American Dream. Briefly, in 1939 two recent Stanford University engineering graduates, Bill Hewlett and David Packard, started the company in a Palo Alto garage with a beginning working capital of $538. They initially marketed an audio oscillator (developed by Bill while at Stanford) that was sold to Walt Disney Studios and adopted for use in the innovative sound system for the movie *Fantasia*. The oscillator, costing less than $100 to produce (one-quarter the price of competitive products), was named the 200A because the founders thought this descriptor would suggest that H-P was a stable company. This collaboration and product birthed both Silicon Valley and the technology revolution.

For almost two decades Hewlett-Packard had no documented market strategy, although there was a strong commitment to electronic test equipment, exceedingly high-quality standards for products, and individual innovation. The company emphasized freedom of action, and words such as "originality" and "novelty" became part of the everyday lexicon. During this period, H-P took contract work as diversified as bowling alley fault-line indicators and harmonic tuners. Most important, however, an internal assessment during the mid-1950s revealed that for most products, sales began to decline and the company's technical advantage began to erode in the fourth year after product introduction. Inadvertently, H-P had uncovered—what are commonly understood today—the S-curve, product growth expectancy, and business maturity cycles. It became evident that if the company intended to increase revenues, it had to generate a steady stream of new ideas, yielding new products. Research and development became the cornerstone for expansion.

By the end of 1957, (1) Bill Hewlett had filed 7 of his 13 patents, (2) the company employed over 1,200 people, and (3) the company had success-fully issued its first public stock. That year the founders took their manage-ment team on a retreat to determine the company's first set of business objectives. The gathering adopted a decentralized model for identifying and developing different products and reinforced the belief that individual initia-tive, experimentation, personal commitment, and caring needed to be culti-vated as essential aspects of the culture. In an era where formal structures and titles were often highlighted by organizations, H-P encouraged collegial interactions, eschewed titles, and, led by its founders, continued to refer to themselves and all employees by their first names. After the meeting, H-P spawned what become known as *The H-P Way*.

As H-P entered the 1990s, the decentralized model and the unleashing of individual inventiveness created a corporate behemoth—multiple divisions with 67 product lines, over 30,000 individual products, $13 billion in rev-enues, and 92,000 employees. In 1997 H-P won an Emmy for its contribu-tions to technologies used for video data and the company became one of the 30 stocks that comprised the Dow Jones Industrial Average (DJIA). By 1998, products ranged from computers and printers to measurement devices to en-gineering components to chemical analysis to medical equipment, revenues exceeded $47 billion, and employment hovered at 124,000. Equally impor-tant, however, H-P concluded that growth had begun to stabilize and that significant changes were occurring in both their competitive markets and customer demands. Accordingly, in 1998 H-P undertook an extensive, for-mal *Growth Initiative*—a nine-month study by the Corporate Strategy Board, internal H-P members, academics, consultants, and members from other cor-porations—to evaluate barriers or stall points to unbroken growth.[1]

A Time of Transition

Beginning in 1999 a number of radical changes occurred:

- H-P spun off a new company named Agilent Technologies, divesting itself of many of its traditional drivers—measurement, component, chemical, and medical businesses.
- H-P appointed its first external chief executive officer (CEO) and presi-dent, Carlton (Carly) S. Fiorina, who had 20 years experience at AT&T and Lucent Technologies.
- H-P disbanded its decentralized structure and introduced a new design based on front-end customer interface functions and back-end product generation functions (i.e., research and manufacturing). The multiple

product lines were compressed into about 25 percent of the original number and increased focus was given to category management and cross-company initiatives.

- H-P strategy began to reemphasize the importance of innovation across three new dimensions: (1) enabling intelligent, connected devices and environments, (2) enabling an always-on Internet infrastructure, and (3) enabling a new generation of appliances delivered as e-service. The H-P logo was changed to *H-P Invent.*
- H-P acquired Compaq Computer Company, thereby increasing revenues to over $70 billion and employment to about 140,000 worldwide. It was the largest merger in technology history. The company, now known as the *New H-P*, became number 1 in several expanding markets, including personal computers, enterprise storage, image and printing, Windows, Linux, and UNIX servers, and management software, as well as number 3 in IT services.
- The final organization was structured into four groups: (1) Enterprise Systems, (2) Imaging and Printing, (3) Services, and (4) Personal Systems. The strategic direction emphasized providing the best return on information technology for business and public customers, providing simple and rewarding experiences to customers, developing a world-class cost structure, and, achieving focused innovations.

The Interview Sample

From December 2002 to January 2003, we conducted interviews with 13 H-P executive leaders and one focus group, which represented a team of 4 senior-level internal consultants who provide strategy consultation to H-P management. Table 2.1 provides their titles and organization at the time of the study. When the interviews were conducted, (1) H-P was immersed in the details of the Compaq integration; (2) global business had been mired in a two-year period of economic instability with low growth, slow demand, and low corporate earnings, and analysts indicated a cautious economic future; and (3) global uncertainty had increased related to post–9/11 events, a potential war with Iraq, corporate scandals, and instability in North Korea. In the technology sector, some analysts characterize the period as a "Technology Winter" —the end of a long positive cycle buoyed by the Internet boom, punctuated by numerous dot-bombs, ending with loss of consumer confidence and an increase in corporate caution. Susan Cook, the VP in Supply Chain Global Operations, stated:

> I think our foresight about what's going to happen in the world is so limited. It's like we're all looking through a haze. We used to stand on top of

Table 2.1

H-P Interview Sample

Name	Title	Business Group
Vyomesh Joshi	EVP	Imaging & Printing Group (IPG)
Debra Dunn	SVP	Office of Corporate Affairs
Dick Lampman	SVP	H-P Research & H-P Labs
John Brennan	SVP	Corporate Office of Strategy & Technology (OS&T)
Barbara Braun	VP	Office of Merger Integration & Strategic Change
Susan Cook	VP	Supply Chain Operations, Global Operations (GO)
Iain Morris	SVP	Mobile Products, Corporate Office of Strategy & Technology (OS&T)
Janice Chaffin	SVP	Marketing & Strategy Solutions, Enterprise Services Group (ESG)
Roger Archibald	VP & GM	Infrastructure and Network and Storage Division, Enterprise Services Group (ESG)
Bob Pearse	VP	Strategy & Business Development, Enterprise Services Group (ESG)
Juletta Broomfield	Director	Alliance & Partners, H-P Services (HPS)
Jose Tormo	Director	Mobile Products, Corporate Office of Strategy & Technology (OS&T)
Doug McGowan	Director & GM	H-P Innovation Centers, Corporate Office of Strategy & Technology (OS&T)
Focus Group		
Sheryl Root	Manager	Internal Strategy Consultant, WW Supply Chain & Customer Operations
Mike Menke	Consultant	Internal Strategy Consultant, Product Process Organization, Global Operations (GO)
Glen Tines	Consultant	Internal Strategy Consultant, Product Process Organization, Global Operations (GO)
Linda White	Consultant	Garage Works

the clear mountain and look out at the valleys, and think we could see all these things that were coming; we had this great view. And now, we're kind of down in a little bunker and it's kind of foggy, and we can't really tell. It's not like we got a global weather system that's going to tell us what's going to happen to the weather.

The Compaq Computer Overlay

Although a focus of this investigation was on the external environmental forces, both the pace of change and the accompanying impact, nearly every interviewee noted the importance of the Compaq merger—an internal factor—as a "lens" for understanding their thinking.[2] Commenting on the magnitude of the merger, Bob Pearse, VP Strategy & Business Development (ESG) suggested:

> You have to separate internal change from external change . . . if you add it all together, this is the biggest period of change and the period of least certainty I've experienced in 20 years of being in this business, without a doubt!

With added emphasis, Barb Braun of the Merger Integration Office remarked that "the acquisition of Compaq Computer Company was a stochastic move, a big shock to the system . . . and the pace of change since then has been very high." An informed comment from Roger Archibald, VP & GM Network and Storage, who had the unique experience of working both for H-P and Compaq before the 2002 close date, focused on the dramatic nature of the merger:

> No company in the world has ever gone through the size of the merger and integration that we're doing right now . . . based on market conditions, the fact that . . . we've got two different business models that we're rolling together . . . this is absolutely the right thing to focus on, because if you don't have it as a foundation, you really are not in a position to execute.

Indeed, most of the comments about the merger focused on the challenges of integrating the two companies—for example, merging the complex infrastructures, selecting and balancing the business portfolio, and determining governance issues. Doug McGowan, General Manager (GM) H-P Innovation Center, discussed the integration period, which played havoc with the internal ecosystem and one's ability to rely on the tried-and-true network:

> The merger has been a huge issue for the company, simply because the amount of work we've had to do in order to figure out what we've got and where we are going . . . it's just really hard and complex. You don't know who is in your eco-system anymore . . . this is the largest merger in high-tech history. So therefore you should have the biggest set of challenges and problems. It's a bit better now, but for a long time you had no idea to whom to go as the whole ecosystem got broken.

A four-person internal strategy consulting team described the integration environment as "sluggish" due to the immensity of the tasks at hand. One focus group member, Linda White, who manages H-P's GarageWorks, added,

"Because we work across the company, I think that part of the slowness that we see is that the integration is so enormously complex . . . it's one thing to put new systems in place and change them and it's another whole thing . . . to change everybody's mental model of how it should work."

A number of respondents, who targeted the acquisition as a major force, emphasized the enormous impact on employees and their ability to cope with the transition. Bob Pearse of Enterprise Services made these observations on the ability to adapt to the acquisition and subsequent integration:

> Certainly the integration has been an incredible change at every level . . . at the strategy, the personal and the cultural level—all of these dramatic changes basically come together—positively and negatively. I'd say the negative is that some people just can't handle this level of change, and they tend to shut down a little bit. The positive side is it's been like an unfreezing event, sort of like the concept of boot camp. When you send someone to boot camp, you totally unfreeze them from where they were. The complete unfreezing is beginning to allow us to re-solidify some things.

Coping with the integration efforts and living with the uncertainty as to where individuals will "end up" in the company was described by Susan Cook:

> I think fear is huge right now for people. I think it exists on a number of different levels, but there is no question that fear about what will happen to us in this merger and will we end up liking where we are—will we like the job that we're going to every day? For example, I see people trusting each other more and helping each other with relationship building, because we kind of know that we're in this together.

Therefore, since H-P was in the midst of the integration during the interview period, it was mentioned by almost half the executives and all the strategy focus group who were actively engaged in integration efforts. The acquisition was a critical part of the H-P strategy—to become number 1 in several key markets—and would be a major force with which to contend regardless of the environmental situation. However, added to the unstable eternal environment, it seemed to exacerbate respondents' perceptions of the environment and their adaptation to it.

External Environmental Forces

During the 13 interviews and one 4-member focus group, we learned which environmental forces were uppermost in the minds of the respondents. Table 2.2

Table 2.2

Environmental Forces

Environmental Forces	
External	Economy
	Technology
	Competition/Focus on Cost/Commoditization
	Customer demand
	Globalization
	Corporate scandals
	Connectedness of capital markets
Internal	Merger with Compaq Computer Co.

indicates the forces, identified in order of the frequency with which they were stated.

The Economy

Many environmental forces were considered to have major impacts on Hewlett-Packard, but the economy was considered the most significant external force by more than half the respondents.[3] In weighing her thoughts about major forces, Janice Chaffin, Senior VP, Marketing & Strategy (ESG), grappled with which force—the merger or economy—was the most significant. Although both were considered major challenges, she presented it with the following positive spin:

> There are two big forces just in the last six months—the merger and the economy slowing down. Everybody's economy has slowed down, it's a worldwide slow-down . . . it really puts the pressure on. So, you can do a merger because nobody is buying anything.

She further added that "when you see [the economic slump] . . . has gone on for a couple of quarters, you realize it's a fundamental shift. It's not just a blip." Iain Morris, SVP of Mobile Products, summed up most of the interviewees' sentiments: "If you had to say, what's one thing that is dramatically driving our business right now, it would have to be the economy at large." Roger Archibald, vice president and general manager, Network and Storage Division, reinforced his colleagues' thoughts and he expressed concern about any uptick in the economy in the near term:

> Obviously the big elephant in the room is the economy. . . . You know, I think people have pretty much come to the conclusion that we're at the bottom,

we're bouncing along the bottom, but there's uncertainty in when we will see any kind of uptick in the economy, and particularly corporate IT spending.

Economic instability was discussed as a worldwide phenomenon with few industries unscathed. "Everybody's economy has slowed down, it's a worldwide slowdown . . . and it really puts the pressure on all of us," succinctly stated by Janice Chaffin, Enterprise Services Group.

In several interviews we learned that the state of the economy produced a number of effects or "pressures" with an increased focus on costs resulting in reduced innovation. For example, Doug McGowan, general manager of H-P's Innovation Centers, asserted that the economy immensely pressured H-P's corporate customers. "CIOs [chief information officers] are mostly concerned with finding ways to cut costs, and are spending less money on innovation unless there's a proven quick ROI [return on investment]. And so that is a big factor in the deployment of new ideas. It hurts us."

Therefore the result of the economic environment was an overall throttling down of IT spending and corporations expecting a return on investments they made during the previous few years. Many enterprise customers had invested—some say overinvested—in the late 1990s in preparation for Y2K, referred to as the millennium bug, and the Internet boom. They were now seeking an appropriate return, according to Jose Tormo, chief strategist for the Mobile Products Group:

> The biggest force that I'm facing right now is economic. Our perception is that our customers overinvested in IT since about '97, '98, when they became afraid of the millennium bug and invested very heavily in new systems with extremely high capacity. They have those systems now. They were told that internet traffic was absolutely exploding, and, as a result, they put in place enormously powerful systems. The result is that typical storage utilization is currently between 25 percent and 30 percent of capacity. Server processor use is running at maybe 30–40 percent of capacity. Desktop processor use is maybe 10 percent of capacity. Ending in late 2000, there was so much supply push for IT infrastructure and PC performance infrastructure that they bought and bought very heavily.

Since H-P's strategy thrives on strong partner relationships, comments were made on the economy's impact on both cost controls and reduced innovation by key partners. According to Juletta Broomfield, a director in Alliance & Partners, "We are in a challenging economic environment. . . . We and our partners are not thinking about incubating new products and services as much as previous years. There is a significant move for partners from a focus on R&D to more billable deliverables."

Additionally, the economy drove the corporation's ability to plan for the long term. According to some interviewees, in the robust, high-growth period preceding this new century, one could plan more effectively. "We used to be able to forecast, with a fairly high degree of accuracy, what was going to happen, from a revenue and a profit perspective, at least the next quarter," according to Debra Dunn, SVP Corporate Affairs. During the period of investigation, several interviewees expressed concern over the short-term mentality that the current economic environment produced.

In closing on the economic environment, another impact was on the individuals themselves. A commentary on one's personal reaction to the slow-growth economy and its impact on the business came from Iain Morris, SVP Mobile Product Group: "If you're in a business that's growing, you can put up with a lot. If you're in a business that's struggling because of economic factors . . . the stress factor is now much greater than it was ten years ago."

Technology

It comes as no surprise that the second major external force for Hewlett-Packard executives was technology. H-P has provided numerous innovations in the technology sector and H-P's growth and overall success are grounded in its technology advances. The birth of the digital age and explosion of digitized information was commented on by several key individuals. Roger Archibald, Enterprise Services Group, summarized his thoughts:

> Today more information is digital than analog, and as a result, the ease in which information now can be distributed and the desire of people to store that information is just exploding huge opportunities . . . this whole trend around going from atoms to bits propagates information . . . as a result of that you get multiple copies of it stored in thousands of places throughout the world.

John Brennan, SVP Corporate Office of Strategy & Technology, suggested that "the creation, capturing, storage and use of information have become more dispersed and prolific . . . and everything we do in the business world is becoming digitized." He continued by underscoring the increasingly prevalent role of technology in business today:

> It's becoming ubiquitous. *Information Technology is business.* You cannot find a single process out there in the world that is not in some way being digitized. It's easy to look at the banking or the telecom industry, and say it's being digitized. Those two industries are all about the manipulation of information. But the real test comes in oil drilling . . . if you go out to an oil drill, you'll find

today that the extraction of natural resources out of the ground is heavily sensored, heavily measured, which creates an absolute torrent of information that needs to be stored and collected and manipulated and managed.

The role of digitization fueled the proliferation of the personal computer and other technologies for personal use. According to Dick Lampman, SVP of H-P Research and Director of well-known H-P Labs:

> For about the last 15 years, technology has been a major force that has led to waves of change in our industry. . . . The widespread acceptance of Unix, which we helped develop, and the arrival of the PC really caused a fault line in the information technology industry. Their arrival was the beginning of more standardization, which allowed the creation of a third-party software industry, which gave us the huge range of applications we have today. This was a pretty epic shift.

With the increased adoption of the personal computer and other consumer technologies, their influence on personal utilization was described by John Brennan:

> In terms of processes being digitized, personal technology will be almost as ubiquitous. The application of technology for personal benefit—whether for pleasure or for productivity—will be extraordinary . . . one only needs to look at cell phone adoption as a good application of that.

Vyomesh Joshi, known as VJ, EVP of the Imaging & Printing Group, emphasized the social aspects of technology advancement: "even though the 'dot-bombs' happened . . . the Internet has continued to evolve . . . the next level of connectedness and mobility actually will drive very interesting dynamics because the social aspect of technology will play a much bigger role." A final comment on the social impact of technology on communications came from Iain Morris, SVP Mobile Products Group:

> A major force is the phenomenal desire for people to be mobile—the lightning bolt is interpersonal communication. I think you will find that man's desire to communicate is what derived the written word—not the spoken word—and in all forms of communication from the smoke signals to drums to film to TV—an insatiable desire to communicate is what drives people to use technology that enables them to be mobile.

Disruptive innovation was also mentioned as a major part of the technology force impacting H-P. According to Bob Pearse, Enterprise Services Group,

"The longest term issues that we tend to worry about are fundamental technology discoveries and technology changes that could really impact just the way we do business today and what we sell today. The trouble with that is that you don't know from where that's going to come." Although H-P drives a significant amount of innovation, vigilance is still required and continual environmental scanning as a technology discontinuity may come unexpectedly from a number of competitors.

John Brennan discussed the technology impact from the vantage point of information technology (IT) being elevated to a key corporate asset, namely a capital expenditure—not to be taken lightly:

> I see one force is technology, which has firmly become the core capital spending of any company. So IT has graduated from being the CIO's accountability with a budget that's largely expense-driven, to being a capital expenditure. So it begins to assume the same role in importance to a company as in the 1930s or 1940s, when you wanted to put up a new factory, you took it all the way to the CEO and then to the board. This is clearly one of the trends that drive the way I think about our strategy.

Therefore, the first two major forces articulated by the H-P executives were the economy and technology and the two were inextricably linked. Economy drives technology innovation and IT spending, and acquired technology is an asset that needs to be effectively utilized. According to Brennan, "If you spent a billion dollars on a steel mill you want to keep it busy. Asset utilization will be a discipline that we apply to information technology going forward—how do you make sure they're used, so that you are using what you're buying and you're not buying more than you need."

The Role of Competition, Focus on Cost, and Commoditization

A major thread that runs through the H-P comments and is linked to both the economy and technology is the role of commoditization as products mature through the adoption life-cycle.[4] With increased competition comes continual cost pressure. Prices become elastic, products become commodities, and revenues shrink. In considering Moore's Law, all this happens at a faster and faster rate.[5] As Doug McGowan, H-P Innovation Centers, suggested, "if you even blink, you can get yourself in trouble." With a focus on innovation and an annual $4 billion investment on research and development, H-P would no doubt consider this a major force with which to contend. Barbara Braun, a principal executive involved in the integration of Compaq at the time of the interview, added:

> I think H-P is subject to a lot of the environmental factors that are global in nature. I think the IT industry has enjoyed many decades of very, very high growth. I think the domestic markets are more saturated. The growth opportunities are in the developing countries. Like many companies, I think as the electronics industry in general commoditizes, competition is increasingly high, which forces you to look at things like how do you produce quality product at the lowest, lowest cost, and deliver it as efficiently as you can to the marketplace. . . . [W]hat's driving the rate of change is the rate at which businesses mature.

According to John Brennan, Office of Strategy & Technology, the competitive pressure is definitely a constant to consider:

> We're not going to see the pressure on cost go away. I think it's reflective of access to capital—the relatively easy access to capital means that companies usually have less grace period in terms of the time between when they introduce a truly differentiated or innovative product, and when their competitors can respond.

Addressing the drive of some competitors to becoming the lowest cost provider, focus group member Glen Tines, senior internal strategy consultant in Global Operations, stated: "When the economy starts to pick up and with the move to commoditization of computing power, all competitors will be scrambling around with the renewed energy to become the lowest cost provider . . . even now there's a great move to become more efficient." Another Global Operations consultant, Mike Menke, known for decision analysis, reflected on the concept of differentiation and the need for close customer linkages: "Whereas in the past, H-P fostered many brilliant proprietary innovations, we have to really struggle. Many of the businesses are just getting to the point of a 'near-commodity.' And so, how do you survive in those kinds of situations? You have to do it by better service, better understanding of customer needs."

Alluding to the need for continuous differentiation in order to remain competitive, John Brennan closed his comments on commoditization with this statement: "With the access to capital means, you just don't have those long, comfortable periods of differentiation. So I don't know if it's the pace of change, but the pace of competition is certainly different."

Customer Demand

With the pressure of containing costs and the increased sophistication of all levels of buyers, customer demand was defined as another key environmental force. The importance of the customer, for whom H-P develops thousands of products and services, was discussed in various ways. Unique to each interviewee was the business the respondent represented and the types of customers each served. Interviewees suggested that customer requirements included the need for simplification and ease of use on the enterprise side to enhanced experience on the consumer front. Bob Pearse of the Enterprise Group explained that customers do not want to deal with the complexity of any product: "Things are getting so complex that people simply want to say, 'I don't care what's in the thing, just put it all together and give me a working automobile. I don't care about the engine.'" Focusing on major corporate customers with significant infrastructures to manage, Dick Lampman, H-P Labs, talked about the need for simplification and the trend toward outsourcing:

> We're finding the complexity and the cost of IT is really pushing customers more and more to want to have less detailed involvement with their IT infrastructures. There's a big push for managed services and outsourcing—we're seeing more customers asking us to help them or run their IT operations for them. More are asking for tools that allow them to run their IT infrastructure more efficiently. In fact, that's where utility computing is coming from. Customers want to take advantage of the thousand computers they have, but the cost of running them exceeds the cost of buying them. They want more agility, to be able to shift their resources, to be able to deploy them more quickly, and they want them more economically.

With a direct purview into enterprise storage and infrastructure customers, Roger Archibald, Network Storage Business, summarized the requirement for simplification, "We [must] consciously figure out a way to make it easier for people to embrace the technology to make it easier to adopt and to deploy."

With a greater focus on the individual and the needs of his imaging and printing consumers, EVP Vyomesh Joshi offered a different perspective. "I always felt that power will come more and more to the individual. . . . [I]f you think about digital imaging, it is all built on experience. Can we create an experience which is very different for our consumers?"

Besides customers wanting differentiated and simplified products and services, H-P considers key partners and strategic alliances into the business equation. Besides keeping customers satisfied, partners also have requirements to be met. Juletta Broomfield, Alliances & Partners, offered, "We need to perform with great flexibility as not all customers want the same things."

Globalization and Connectedness

Issues surrounding globalization echoed throughout the H-P interviews, including the worldwide economic impact ("a worldwide slowdown"), the role of technology (its development and utilization), and the current geopolitical conditions including post–September 11, 2001, events. Although these forces were identified separately in Table 2.2, interviewees tended to speak of them in tandem; therefore, we have combined them for our ongoing discussion.

After H-P merged with Compaq Computer Corporation in May 2002, H-P's presence expanded to 178 countries, doing business in 40+ currencies and in a minimum of 10 languages.[6] Before and after the acquisition, H-P had great global presence and, therefore, had significant reactions to global events. Due to her global charter and continued worldwide focus, Debra Dunn, Corporate Affairs, commented extensively on H-P's proactive role in global affairs and the impact of global dynamics on the corporation:

> The 9/11 incident certainly had impact on the business community in many, many ways. It impacted some of the work that we're specifically driving . . . and it ratcheted up our concern about the fundamental instability in the environment in which we operate. We're very global . . . and our business growth and success is partly dependent upon enough health and stability in that global context—to allow us to continue to grow and thrive far beyond the borders of the country.

In discussing globalization, geopolitical issues related to homeland security were raised by several leaders as technology plays a significant role for all types of markets and sectors. For example, Dick Lampman of H-P Labs stated:

> There's a lot of interest in the public sector right now about homeland security issues. That's sort of the micro trend, but it's certainly obvious that the public-sector people are looking for technology capability to do it in a very aggressive way. In fact, my next appointment is with the CIO with the Department of Defense. . . . And we've been getting more visitors like that in considerable numbers.

VJ, Imaging & Printing Group, reviewed geopolitical pressures and security issues related to increased terrorism. He also introduced two additional forces—market connectedness and corporate ethics—to be covered later in this section.

> The whole current political situation—from 9/11 on—has completely changed. . . . [T]hat brings a lot of very interesting challenges, from per-

sonal security to corporate security issues. . . . [T]he whole capital environment is completely changed . . . the connectedness of the financial markets
now and the right business ethics are creating very interesting dynamics,
where companies will have to go back to the basics.

Building on VJ's comments, several other leaders went beyond geopolitical events to emphasize the connected nature of business. Although having
been an international company for almost half a century,[7] H-P's global role
continues to increase by addressing needs of emerging markets, "making
sure we've got a broad spectrum of products able to address emerging countries as well as the traditional U.S. and European economies," according to
Roger Archibald.

The instant communication that occurs between all parts of the globe and
the increased technical competencies outside the United States has influenced the thinking and planning of H-P leaders. As markets are global, the
creation and production of innovative products and services have migrated
to other geographies. According to Susan Cook, Global Operations Supply
Chain Organization:

> We believe that the globalization of the economy is going to have a radical,
> radical change on the way that we produce products and services in our
> company. An example is the way service has moved to Asia. Or the way
> design is coming from Taiwan, India, and China . . . and as things get
> outsourced, if we've outsourced manufacturing, we've outsourced service,
> now if we outsource engineering that will be another huge change for H-P.

Being connected 24×7 by technology of all types—computers with instant message capability, cell phones, PDAs, etc.—has allowed us to have
immediate communication worldwide. There are great benefits to the increased
connectedness, which extends the corporate need to understand a broader,
more complex set of customer needs and issues. Barb Braun, Merger Integration Office, addressed the globalization challenges this way:

> The way that business is done is going to continue to change really rapidly,
> particularly with the globalization of the world and, in particular, with the
> wealth acquisition of developing countries, I think things will continue to
> change really rapidly. So I just can't help but think that a lot of the old
> norms are not going to be as viable or relevant as they were.

In summary, many of the global issues that were mentioned were considered challenges to the corporation. But globalization was also seen as pro-

viding enormous opportunities for H-P in emerging markets. For example, VJ commented:

> We have a tremendous opportunity in emerging markets in India, China, in Eastern Europe, where they will jump the technology curve because they don't have to go through what developed countries do. For example, you can get connectivity way faster there, because you can skip the land lines and go straight to wireless technology. I think we are going to see that the adoption rate of some of our products, like digital imaging, will be way faster in emerging economies.

Several interviewees also suggested that the world does not act in as predictable a fashion as three to five years ago. An ability to understand global dynamics and what they mean for the technology sector is critical to success. Susan Cook stated her organization's challenge: "One of the big strategic issues for our organization is to understand what some of those global trends are and how we're going to respond and help H-P respond." As the world becomes more connected and markets shift, the need to increase agility was a critical success factor mentioned by H-P leaders.

Corporate Scandals

During the investigation we heard references to corporate scandals,[8] prevalent during the interview period. Several comments were heard about the need for a "back-to-basics" approach in light of multiple ethical challenges facing global corporations. The essence of this conversation was captured by Debra Dunn, SVP Corporate Affairs:

> The corporate scandals in the United States have been very significant in raising the profile and emphasis around our strategies in the area of standards of business conduct.... It's been fascinating to watch the change in the image of business leaders in this country over the last couple of years.... I think we're not going to see the end of that.... H-P always has and does now view our role as much broader. We've always thought we existed, not to make a profit but to make a contribution to the communities we're part of.

The Pace of Change and Sense of Turbulence: Still Crazy After All These Years?

> *"What has been is what will be, and what has been done is what will be done; there is nothing new under the sun."*
> —Ecclesiastes 1:1–11

In exploring beyond the boundary of the forces themselves, interviewees were asked how the environment felt from a comparative "pace" and "turbulence" perspective. Is it faster, more dramatic and, if so, why? Respondents differed in how they compare the current environment to past experiences and offered varying opinions on the concept of "turbulence." We heard comments as succinct as "in terms of change, it's much faster" (Barb Braun) to much more calibrated responses as from Janice Chaffin, SVP of Marketing & Strategy Solutions:

> I think "turbulent" is a good description, but that would almost imply that it's going to settle down. I don't think it will. If you think you're going through rough waters and you're going to get to calm waters, those days are gone, forever . . . everything's happening 24 hours a day, seven days a week, around the globe. So, I don't know what the right word is. It's just that everything is in real time, and you can't stop because there may be impacts on your business if you stop. It has all sorts of implications for human beings, to be honest—a fairly dramatic shift.

Along similar lines but questioning whether times have changed or it is merely our perception of it, Bob Pearse, Enterprise Services Group, summed it this way:

> If you add it all together, this is the biggest period of change and the period of least certainty I've experienced in 20 years of being in this business, without a doubt. The only reason I pause on that is that it seems like every time I talked to someone at any point in time over the last 20 years, people said exactly that. And so I'm just wondering if maybe it's always a point of view people have.

Reflecting on the past ten years and promoting the argument that the environment has not radically changed from the past, Iain Morris, Mobile Products, stated:

> I spent my career working in semiconductors and the communications and IT business. It's equally turbulent and equally stressful and equally demanding since I can recall. Now I think that the peaks and troughs increased; this is the worst downturn in the history of the world . . . but I think the confusion, uncertainty, and the chaos continues to exist as it did ten years ago. I really don't remember working less hard 10 years ago!

Reinforcing the line of thought that the environment has not become more chaotic, VJ, the EVP of Imaging & printing, said, "If you think about it, the turbulent times are not new. If you read about the industrial revolution, the same kind of chaos existed there." Additionally, John Brennan, Corporate Strategy, opined that corporations no longer have long comfortable periods to differentiate themselves, but he did not believe that it was attributable to the "pace of change" but the pace of the competition:

> If we break this down into the pace of competition and the pace of product development, Yes, they are faster. The pace of customer decision-making? No, that's not necessarily faster. . . . I don't think there's anything funda-mental about people making decisions faster today than they did years ago. I think in response to cyclical requirements a couple of years ago, people made decisions quickly because they felt like their competitors were getting ahead of them.

In a completely antithetical direction, Doug McGowan, H-P Innovation Centers, described the environment as actually having slowed down rather than accelerated:

> Actually, I think for our industry . . . the pace of change has slowed down, because where in the 'dotcom' era, we had a very high pace of change, people trying new business models and almost anything being funded by a VC [venture capitalist] somewhere . . . things were happening fast. Now, it's sort of a consolidation. Things have slowed down somewhat. Now, the competitive pressures are still huge. . . . But people are more back to the "tried and true" with business models and proven technology.

Executives had clear preferences on terminology to describe the environ-ment. When asked about the pace of change and the sense of turbulence and/or chaos, the Global Operations VP Susan Cook described the environment, tem-pered by the element of predictability: "There's always stuff coming out of left field. But at the same time, I don't think 'chaos' is the right term. It really isn't. There's still some predictability here. For example, we still report earnings every quarter." Debra Dunn, Corporate Affairs, debated terminology given her sense of the current environment, "Turbulence is an interesting word. And it probably isn't the word that I would use to characterize what's been so differ-ent about the last year or so. Uncertainty is more the difference."

With another challenge to terminology, John Brennan disagreed with the concept of "pace of change" and suggested that decisions and actions should not be accelerated unless the pace of the customer changes:

> I think there's a lesson in this so-called pace of change . . . that's been written about so much in terms of organizational development and strategy

setting. It's created this whole kind of furor around everything is faster and everything is faster. Well, I think if you went back and back-tested and talked to people about the decisions they were forced to make quickly, most of them would have been better off if the decision had completely passed them by and they hadn't done anything because in more than one occasion their decisions were wrong. . . . To my way of thinking, one needs to keep one's eye on customers and the people who, in essence, are consumers of your products or services, and ask "at what pace are they changing?"

Adaptation to the Pace and Sense of Turbulence

In considering the impact of the environment—unprecedented to some executives—several leaders commented on how individuals needed to adapt to the increasing environmental demands. For example, increased flexibility was articulated as one success factor by Debra Dunn:

> We, as a company, have never operated in an environment of so much uncertainty on so many fronts. . . . I think that impacts strategy by making you . . . constantly reassess, review, reprioritize, and you need to really ratchet up the agility even more.

She continued to express the need for adaptation to the changing environment: "You've got to be ready to respond. So that requires a high tolerance for ambiguity, excellent stress management skills, and agility across the organization which most large organizations aren't accustomed to." Similarly, Susan Cook discussed the impact of the pace of change on the employee: "I think fear and uncertainty about the world is so much greater than it ever has been before, and I think that is changing the way what we think about our options—between economic uncertainty, political uncertainty, war, everything. People are behaving very, very differently within the company than they did five years ago."

Throughout the interview process, the current environment was described as turbulent, uncertain, unprecedented, and/or the same or different to past experiences. Although various coping mechanisms were suggested, one interviewee, Dick Lampman of H-P Labs, believed that change is a constant that needs to be embraced. He focused on change as a significant part of his organization's charter: "I'm in the change business, that's what I do for a living —what we think about all the time is change." He implied that the corporation must keep a watch on the changes occurring and even drive the changes so that they will maintain the number 1 position in most key markets.

Strategy at Hewlett-Packard

The beginning of the investigation focused on two primary issues and their relationship during this unique period in history. Those issues—strategic management and environmental impacts—reveal an interesting story at Hewlett-Packard. Given the two previous years that ended a period of unmatched progress of the 1990s, the idea of crafting strategy began to take a backseat for some corporate leaders.[9] Was this the case for H-P? How were H-P leaders thinking strategically while contending with the multiple environmental forces and a significant merger? Was there a difference in strategic thinking and strategy formulation now as compared to the H-P of the previous half century?

Evolution of H-P Strategy

At its conception and for 20 years, H-P was in start-up mode, revealing the entrepreneurial and innovative orientation of its founders. Both had a very practical foundation, having spent their college and early work years in the throes of the Depression. Although they had decided to form their own business after their undergraduate years at Stanford, Dave Packard took a job at General Electric in 1935 as jobs and money were scarce and it would give them a knowledge and financial advantage when they did begin their company. In 1937 Bill and Dave had their first official business meeting covering "tentative organization plans and work program for proposed business venture" with products including high-frequency receivers and medical equipment.[10] Early in its organizational lifecycle, H-P was focused on innovating quality products and establishing a sound customer base. They also developed a firm constituent base—colleagues from Stanford, MIT, and General Electric, including Charlie Litton, Russ Varian, and Fred Terman. This nucleus of relationships inspired product development as well as manufacturing capabilities in Palo Alto. It seemed from the beginning that Bill and Dave had a way of acting and making decisions that was considered different from prevailing management strategies of the 1940s and 1950s that focused primarily on profits and revenue growth. For Bill and Dave, business success also included the following:

- a focus on fields of interest in which innovative, meaningful contributions were possible;
- a dedicated, fairly compensated workforce and a work environment that fostered intense individual creativity;
- a company-wide commitment to community involvement.[11]

According to Dave, "Our rapid growth up to 1956 had brought to light some organizational weaknesses. And with prospects for continuing growth ahead, I thought it was time to provide more structure to the company and a better delineation of goals and responsibilities."[12] The company was maturing and progressing through its organization lifecycle, requiring more order and a clearer statement of direction. In 1957, 20 senior H-P managers went to the Sonoma Mission Inn to "discuss policies and problems, to exchange views, and to make plans for the future." Dave drafted a set of corporate objectives that were presented to gain agreement on a common direction. A second version of the objectives was published in 1966 and formed the basis of the H-P Way—the values and strategic foundation of H-P.[13]

In assessing the strategic thinking during the early years, there were several consistent elements. First, driven by the experience of the Depression years, H-P did not incur any long-term debt. Most profits were reinvested into R&D, plus funds from employee stock purchase helped finance growth. Also stock was retained in order to acquire other companies by exchange rather than outright purchase. Acquisitions began in 1958 to build product lines. A system to measure the success of new products was developed and was represented by five-year vintage charts. This approach to strategic management was a constant for H-P for the next 20 years, while Bill and Dave were H-P's driving forces. However, new methods for thinking strategically began to develop as new leadership succeeded Bill and Dave. In 1977, John Young became president and was assigned the additional role of CEO the following year. His focus was on operational excellence and he spearheaded a number of quality improvement efforts such as TQC (Total Quality Control) at H-P.

Ten-Step Business Planning Process

In 1984, John Doyle, leading H-P's R&D, was chartered to develop a new strategic and business planning process. He hired Scott Feemster from Atari to drive the development of a process called the Ten-Step Business Planning Process, which was initially outlined on one page. Business Units were initially approached with just one step—Step 3: the Customer with a focus on the Channel added later. This approach was decided as it seemed to be the missing link in H-P's strategic thinking and approach to planning.[14] *Fortune* magazine published an article in October 1984 that highlighted the new emphasis on planning strategically with the customer at the forefront.[15] Jan Dekema, one of the long-term team members responsible for design and maintenance of Ten-Step, also reported that Doyle encountered Michael Porter's *Competitive Strategy* written in 1980. As a result, the book was disseminated and became the text of choice to accompany the Ten-Step approach for many H-P leaders.

In July 1990, John Young, then H-P's CEO, stated:

> In the 1990s HP will need to seek growth opportunities with a great deal of insight and skill. We can grow in two different ways—by building on capabilities and successes we've already achieved and by innovating new technologies and entering entirely new markets. The Ten-Step planning process will help us identify those opportunities.[16]

For almost 20 years, H-P supported the use of the Ten-Step Process throughout all divisions and multiple product lines. An introduction to the Ten-Step approach outlines key strategic elements.

> At its heart, strategy is about making choices. Choosing who your customers are . . . what solutions you intend to provide, and how you want to deliver value to your customers are all elements of strategy. If the organization is unable or unwilling to engage in these choices, do not expect the planning process to result in strategy.[17]

Specifically, the Ten-Step Process was defined as a way of looking at the business environment and making strategic decisions. It included a planning framework with both a format for articulating content and a set of methodologies for drawing conclusions. According to a white paper describing the approach, "this framework has been the cornerstone of business planning for many organizations throughout H-P since the 1980's."[18]

The Ten Steps, evolved from a University of Sussex UK project, was outlined as follows:

Step 1: Statement of Purpose
Step 2: Five-Year Objectives
Step 3: Customers and Channels
Step 4: Competition
Step 5: Ideal Solution and Strategy
Step 6: Implementation
Step 7: Financial Analysis
Step 8: External Assumptions
Step 9: Internal Interdependencies
Step 10: First-Year Plan

The planning process emphasized the balance between internal and external focus and strategic versus tactical or operational efforts. There was a working order to the process with feedback loops and validation suggested. Figure 2.1 maps the process flow and indicates the role of building focus, understanding the opportunities, making decisions, and implementation.

Over time, the process developed an aura of structured methodology, complete in itself. One might believe that by doing these ten steps, the organization's plan was documented and ready to execute. However, in examining further descriptive Ten-Step documents, we found a planning guide that addressed the continuous nature of the planning process:

> Although known as the Ten-Step business planning process, its proper application actually requires twelve steps. "Step 0" has been added to get organizations to review their rationale for planning in order to increase the likelihood of an effective process. In addition, "Step 11," which in the past was part of Step 10, has been purposely isolated as a stand-alone step to emphasize the importance of a continuous planning discipline.[19]

Jan Dekema, one of the team members engaged in developing and maintaining the Ten-Step process, reported that there was great emphasis placed on the customer and channel to insure greater attention to both groups and delivering better results to and through them.[20] However, one step alone does not yield a strategy. It is probably due to this initial emphasis that we found the following caveat:

> It is the process of going through the entire Ten-Step framework, rather than within a specific step, that creates an organization's strategy. The logic underlying the strategy is built through a series of insightful analyses performed in the sequence of steps and approached in a linked and iterative manner. . . . It is necessary to work through this framework holistically rather than in considering any step in isolation.[21]

Although Ten-Step was supported by H-P in the 1980s as the business planning process,

> Its use as a process for making key strategic decisions at the business unit level was never mandated but recommended. What was mandated was the Ten-Step format to summarize a unit's plan of record (the BSS, the Business Strategy Summary) that, in turn, was submitted in the annual strategy review process (BSR, Business Strategy Review). As a decision making tool, Ten-Step was used in some businesses and not in others. Where it was used was often modified by the local management.[22]

Figure 2.1 **Ten-Step Planning Process**

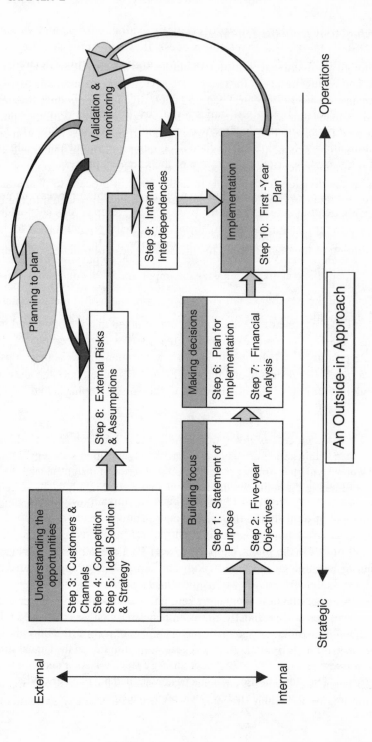

Moving Away from the Ten-Step Approach

Although not mandated, Ten-Step Planning was a diehard part of H-P's planning and review mind-set for two decades. However, through this period the company was very decentralized and each division or product line developed its plans that were aggregated at the corporate level. With the entrance of a new CEO in 1999, the company began to move to a more corporate-conscious environment that thought and acted as a more integrated company. Strategic decisions were crafted at the Executive Committee rather than at the division leader level. In 2001–2002, a process to plan strategically and review progress on a continuous basis was presented to the business units. The process, referred to as Strategic Planning and Review (SPaR), was based on benchmarking strategic planning processes at like-companies in addition to leveraging H-P's historically successful practices. The difference from previous planning approaches was the corporate-wide nature of the plans that were aimed at measuring and projecting performance as well as determining whether or not H-P as a corporation would meet profitability and shareholder value objectives. The SPaR process included a more formal, semiannual review process so that a deeper understanding of business unit strategies, execution plans, and results could be communicated. In addition, a strategy council was established to monitor strategic and technology issues that arose throughout the year where action needed to be taken on a more continuous basis.

Reflections on Strategy Formulation: Interview Findings

During the three- to four-year period prior to the investigation, H-P experienced major changes, including a shift in executive leadership, a reinvention initiative, a reorganization to a front-back organization model, a move to implement several major cross-company initiatives, and an attempt to acquire Price Waterhouse Consulting, all major transitions by themselves. In the fall of 2001, the major decision to acquire Compaq Computer was announced and strategic decision-making and action were wrapped around planning for the integration of two major industry players. Several months later, in the throes of planning the integration, interviews with senior leaders commenced. When considering the question of how strategy was done, H-P leaders thought about it in various ways. The greatest number focused on the process itself and the changes that occurred in strategy formulation over the recent past.

To begin, we focus on what is strategy and then how it was managed during this period. John Brennan, SVP Corporate Strategy & Technology, offered this definition of strategy and suggested the significance that it plays in driving H-P decisions:

> Strategy is the collective of decisions we make about which new products, which new market, how we bring those products to market, and how we organize to bring those products to market—a collective set of decisions that we make to either enter markets, and just as importantly, the choices we make not to do things.

Dick Lampman, H-P Labs, responded with this description of the strategy process, in which he suggests the need for flexibility and a truly interactive process with the customer.

> I think the fundamentals don't change. I think one of the key things—and I think there's been some evidence of this in the business literature—is that good strategy development cannot be a truly top-down, inflexible process; it has to be a living thing. It has to have good listening in it that's tapping the best minds in the organization, and that's proactively building insightful connections into the customer world.

Janice Chaffin, SVP Enterprise Marketing & Strategy, also supported the idea that strategy is not a deterministic but an iterative process: "I think that one of the things that is changing perhaps is that strategy is more a general path or direction that seems about right and that you constantly are adjusting and recommitting to it, as you learn more." She went on to support the notion that leadership style and experience drives how strategy is developed:

> It's both formal and informal. . . . What I have personally found is that it depends on the leadership style . . . that certain leaders, because of their experience and background will gravitate to one method. . . . If people are big-picture thinkers who want to get results, they will start with strategy. If someone is the great tactician, they will do strategy last. . . . I think you never want to get too far in either camp, to be honest . . . you have to have a blend to make it work. . . . for instance, if the person who loves to start with strategic perspectives spends way too much time there, you will fail. The business will fail because the real world isn't going to give you time to plug every hole and get every answer.

Leaning more toward rigorous approach with intermittent assessment, Debra Dunn, SVP Corporate Affairs, said, "I think the thing that's critical is having a level of rigor around the strategic thought applied to the major businesses and having a mechanism to test that thought and that rigor at periodic intervals."

Strategy Starting Point—The Market and Customers

There was resonance among several H-P leaders on their starting point in crafting strategy, namely, the external market environment. VJ, executive leader for the Imaging & Printing Group—the major H-P profit engine—outlined his thoughts on the critical role of the market and the customer: "We start with the market. We size the market, look at the growth rate of the market, understand the customer needs in two ways: first, their current needs, how are they satisfied with what we are doing or how are they unsatisfied. . . . Second, talk about their problems and how we can solve those problems with technology or a better business model solution."

Similar to the comments made by VJ and supporting the need for the continuous external purview, Iain Morris, Mobile Products, reported: "The strategic process that we have employed over a number of years now encompasses a significant amount of customer and market knowledge that we have and competitive knowledge that we collect." With continued attention on the marketplace, and continuous need to adjust as change occurs, Janice Chaffin, Enterprise Marketing, stated:

> You need to constantly have a flow of information as the marketplace is constantly moving and never sleeping. Things are happening hourly that you need to deal with . . . it's not just strategy, it's pretty much every part of your business has to be able to adjust and course-correct. You have to make big decisions on a real-time basis.

The need for continual active exchange with the customer was described by John Brennan, Corporate Strategy, who focused on customer needs and requirements as a key underpinning of strategic thinking:

> I think the great learning from this whole Internet period was some of the big companies were the winners, because they continued to talk to customers and asked them what they really wanted. And there were lots of little companies who got access to capital, who got a better idea, who created a lot of increase in the pace of competition, and they did a lot in terms of the pace of product development. But fundamentally their strategies were out of step with what their customers wanted. They need to move as fast as the customer segments move in terms of anticipating new things, and to reflect what competitors are doing and the like. But, it turns out that the great failure over the last couple of years was to keep looking over your shoulder at your competitors and forget about what your customers wanted or didn't want.

Brennan summed up the importance of a customer-focused strategy in this way, "From an external perspective, what really are our customers asking for? What do we see as the significant, unmet . . . unanticipated customer requirement that will in essence be the driving force going forward for that particular business unit?"

Along with the best market understanding, comments were made by Debra Dunn, Corporate Affairs, on the internal capability of being flexible, that is, making real-time decisions and the trade-offs required while developing strategy:

> We're in a very turbulent environment from the perspective of uncertainty of what's happening externally. The economic environment is volatile and uncertain. The global environment on many dimensions is volatile and uncertain. And what I think that means is, you need to look at strategy a little bit differently. So, I think strategies tend to be fairly long term if they're done in the right way, in that they point you in a certain direction that help you align priorities. But I think today more than ever, we need to be pretty fluid to make real-time trade-offs, to be agile within the context of the broader strategy to respond to things that may not have been anticipated.

Scenario Thinking Augments Strategy

During periods of uncertainty, one aspect of strategy development that becomes more useful is the development of scenarios, which requires a different type of strategic thinking, but provides various alternative views of the future. Bob Pearse of Enterprise Services suggested this approach to keeping an eye on future possibilities: "There's tremendous potential change that's occurring in the marketplace, therefore, we've engaged with folks around processes like scenario planning . . . to be able to lay out different plausible scenarios for what might happen in the future that—if they happen—could totally change the way they look at their business."

Identifying early warning signals and an approach to being proactive on an ideal scenario was Susan Cook, VP Supply Chain Operations:

> We also have done a lot of scenario planning. For example, during the merger, we did some strategic planning, and came up with 11 different scenarios that we thought were possible for H-P and for our organization. We then narrowed that down to four that we thought were the most likely. We created a trigger mechanism that . . . would tell us that this was going to happen. And then, if that happened, we actually chose a most

desirable scenario, and said, "if that was the scenario we wanted to have happen, what would we have to do to try to influence the outcome to make that happen?"

Juletta Broomfield, H-P Services, offered a perspective on scenarios as a rational approach to thinking strategically: "The scenario process helped us to reduce distraction and emotion." Although scenario development was done at H-P at various other stages, normally it was valued during times of turbulence and uncertainty. During the integration period, it is of interest that the request for scenario work increased markedly.

Different Strategy Approaches Pre-Merger

In addressing the integration of Compaq into the H-P fold, some leaders commented on the difference between H-P and Compaq in areas of planning and strategic thinking prior to the acquisition. Holding a dual perspective, as he worked at both H-P and Compaq at various times, Roger Archibald, Enterprise Services Group, compared the two companies based on the formal versus informal formulation approach:

> If I look at pre-merger Compaq and pre-merger H-P, Compaq had much less formal process than it was at H-P. And at H-P, we had a very rigorous Ten-Step business planning process that was uniformly adopted across the business group that I was part of and that we used to drive that process going forward. The content was very similar in both places, but the way that Compaq got pulled together in the presentation of it was much less structured.

During the dialog with a focus group of internal consultants, providing strategy guidance to vice presidents and general managers, Glen Tines reported on the difference between the two companies—one more centralized yet the second more formal in its planning processes:

> From the H-P side, there was more focus on process and structured methods for doing business planning and strategy development. Plans were primarily developed in distinct, independent business groups—it was a decentralized model. . . . Compaq seemed to be more centralized, highly relationship-driven and much more action oriented. Some from Compaq would say 'shoot from the hip" was a preferred method for planning.

Commenting on the differences in pre- and post-acquisition H-P, Barb Braun, Merger Integration Office, outlined planning for the acquisition and, subsequently, planning once the close occurred. She discussed the move to a more classic approach once the close was finalized and the two companies were one:

> Prior to the purchase of Compaq Corporation, we had a strategic planning process. The process of buying and integrating Compaq caused us basically to apply a very, very different process to plan, what we call The New Company. . . . [W]e're now implementing for this first round, a more traditional business planning or strategy planning in the new company, applying some of the old tools that we have in our tool kit. And I anticipate, as we move out of this first period, we will probably fairly dramatically change our planning process. So, I mean, the strategic planning process really, right now, is a fairly classic process.

Alignment

Besides strategy development processes, other key strategic elements were raised. Many of these following elements are interdependent but will be first described separately. Due to the scale of H-P's product and solution reach, issues of complexity were discussed and the success factors required in managing the enterprise. As a result, alignment of key internal contributors was seen as a critical success factor in the crafting of strategy. "H-P is a quite broad company in terms of its focus, and so, when you're trying to link and align across a pretty broad landscape, that's challenging on many dimensions. It's challenging in terms of the time and energy required to keep the right people in the various parts of the organization connected at the right level," according to Debra Dunn, Corporate Affairs. She continued to discuss the ongoing need for internal alignment due to the challenges, outlined in the previous environmental force dialogue:

> Five years ago there really wasn't an attempt to think broadly across the whole portfolio and say "given this portfolio, what is our overarching strategy?" I think the change has something to do with leadership and has a lot to do with the environment that we're operating in, and what it's going to take to achieve our aspiration of being THE technology leader. We don't think we can get there without having alignment around what the overall strategy of the company is.

VJ, the EVP from Imaging & Printing, reinforced the need for internal alignment, namely, continual dialog and feedback in the crafting of strategy:

> I spend a lot of time with my staff, at my various sites and with the regions. . . . I do a lot of strategy through conversation and everybody really

helps us because the future is always fuzzy. But when you bring in smart people and smart partners you really make it very, very clear. And then we talk about future but come back to the present, and then start working on what we will achieve this week, then this month, then this year.

Responsible for a unique horizontal function, Susan Cook, Supply Chain Operations, talked about the need for being relationship focused with primary customers and balancing the insights by monitoring external environment:

> We do a lot of networking and relationship building with people. . . . [O]rganizationally we have the top 20 relationships we think we need; we go out and we talk to those people and figure out what their business issues are. We do a lot of external scanning.

From well-established H-P Labs, Dick Lampman outlined the contribution of a broad range of professionals with deep domain knowledge who craft strategy iteratively with a common strategic direction in mind:

> Strategy has to exist in the framework of real ideas and real insight. For that part of the process is the contribution of various research leaders and various technical contributors; it is typically an iterative process. At the end of the day, it's really all completely dependent on the quality of people you've got and we have some really great people . . . it's building a common vision that attracts people to it and it's shifting resources to it to make it happen.

Furthermore, Lampman emphasized the necessary alignment required between H-P Labs and the business units, whom the lab serves:

> One of our key roles is to engage in the development of company strategy and we do that for two reasons: one of which is to understand the current strategy to give our research leadership and teams a better understanding of the overall business and customer environment. And then, reciprocally, our intention is to shape those strategies as we understand technology forces and technology issues which are emerging.

From a different enterprise perspective, representing the infrastructure and storage organization, Roger's Archibald discussed the balancing act between strategy formulation and execution: "Our role as a staff is to set the fundamental direction, but with a context around it, so that when people start to execute that strategy, it gets better because there it is more applied—not to change the direction but to refine it and then execute."

Another element that enhances strategy formation and strategic thinking is continuous external dialogue with customers, partners, and other thought leaders as emphasized by Bob Pearse, ESG:

> We spend a lot of time looking for consensus, externally to see what's going on—looking for people whom we normally wouldn't talk to—in order to understand things and to avoid breathing our own exhaust. So I spend as much as I can in our visitor center, talking to customers, and actually much more time with those from Asia Pacific, India, and Europe because America is one area from which we get a little more regular feedback. So I'm trying to look at different points of view.

In summarization, alignment requires internal and external knowledge and relationships as well as a keen understanding of the customer needs and wants as stated by Archibald:

> I think it's a blend of a number of things. Obviously we're tracking very closely the technology, the technology trends, and the enabling capabilities of technology. We are highly engaged with partners and so the collaboration with partners and emerging companies is something that's a key part of our strategy development. And, then, thirdly is the overall analysis of user needs and customer wants, desires, and the challenges that they are faced with.

The Centralized Versus Decentralized Organization

Historically H-P has been known as a decentralized organization, designed with minimal corporate structure and with multiple product lines—each an independent division. The rationale of H-P's transition from a decentralized to a more centralized structure and the renewed approach to strategy was summarized by Lampman, director of H-P Labs:

> The company came from a pretty long tradition of a very highly decentralized business model, and, if anything, that probably reached its zenith in the mid to late 1990s. And while that model actually worked very well for us in the past, both in the early days of the company and even in the period since we got into computer systems, in a lot of ways it fundamentally broke down as we found ourselves in systems businesses, which required more integration and a more intensely competitive environment, which required a lot more leveraging of the assets that we have.

The need for alignment across major product categories in order to enhance customer experience was another reason for moving to a more centralized structure as described by Debra Dunn, Corporate Affairs:

> Five or six years ago, H-P was still quite heavily decentralized around the product division, and there were eighty-ish of those. In the computer systems business, there was a need for very, very tight interconnection and alignment across the division strategies in that organization. But in a lot of other businesses, there was less of a focus on getting the strategies aligned. So there was less rigor around corporate-level strategy. A couple of things have shifted that approach. One is based on what's happening in our world and with technology—there's more linkage in every dimension. Increasingly we're looking at compatibility between products across the entire business, so we want the consumer experience to be a very simple and intuitive experience.

Bob Pearse talked about unifying the businesses in order to capitalize on the power of H-P across its portfolio. At the time of the investigation and the move to a more centralized approach, more cross-company initiatives began to appear:

> Several years back there was no real corporate strategy, we didn't really have a top-down view, a top-down strategy, we were a bunch of individual business units, each going our own merry way. . . . So the strength of what we're doing today at the corporate level—almost a complete 180 to where we were nine years ago—was primarily driven by a recognition of a failure in H-P to take advantage of our strengths across the different business units. In other words, we were still acting as a bunch of individual business units, and at the same time we were missing some key trends and key issues that went across all of the business units.

One could argue that a move to centralization was also a move to improved alignment. By becoming more centralized, businesses could begin to act as one in order to make more of a business impact on customers and better contend with competitors. Brennan, Corporate Strategy Office, remarked that "The last couple of years have been the years of lots of transition in H-P—much less decentralized. We're looking for a little bit more corporate involvement because H-P had traditionally left a lot on the table, particularly from the perspective of the leverage between the business units." Barb Braun, Merger Integration Office, commented on the one company approach and its intended focus on better serving customer needs.

> The operating model, which Hewlett-Packard has specifically adopted, is that we are one company. However, we have dependent assets that we will

all use to create a collective, competitive advantage on two things. One is having one face to our customers and being able to service our customers' macro needs, and second is efficiency in the delivery of our goods and services.

The role of leadership in a centralized organization may connote an ivory-tower approach to some observers; however, Janice Chaffin, Enterprise Services Group, believed that even with corporate attention to strategy formulation, H-P leaders are pragmatic:

> We have people who have been in, built, managed, operated real businesses, so they might be good at thinking broadly and doing critical analysis, but they're practical. We think that has helped in a huge number of ways, because we don't have a lot of ivory-tower people coming up with stuff that just can never happen—the things that we come up with are achievable, doable but stretch us . . . we're not way off the mark when we talk about strategy. If there's a weakness, it's sticking to a strategy. . . . I think you have to have the leadership commitment to stick to something long enough, but to do the opposite also—when something is not working, to make a change quickly.

With a history of innovation with a decentralized organization, what happens to innovation in the new centralized organization design? John Brennan disagreed with the potential negative impact on innovation: "I don't totally accept the notion that greater central control has diminished innovation. I don't think we've diminished innovation . . . some of the smaller innovations have been sacrificed . . . but I would be the first to point out to you that the central strategy process has actually saved some innovations for much longer than they might have otherwise been saved."

Because H-P has moved to a more centralized model, are the businesses managed in the same way and with the same business model? VJ, leading Imaging & Printing, described H-P as having multiple business models and highlighted two within his business:

> In the imaging and printing business, we have two very different business models, one with Inkjet—we have a proprietary technology that we developed bottoms up—and for LaserJet, we chose a partnership strategy, where we worked with our partner, Canon. We have actually evolved both models over the last 18 years. What we have done very systematically is to have a very clear strategic planning process. I think we have the most rigorous strategic planning process in H-P.

Planning Cycle

Another aspect of strategy that was described by H-P leaders was the planning cycle. Prior to the change in executive leadership and the major Compaq acquisition, H-P's planning occurred on an annual cycle with the routinized ten-step planning approach done by all the product lines and divisions. With major changes in the corporation and the overall environment, planning processes and cycles began to shift as well. The revised planning process and annual cycle was outlined by John Brennan, who has accountability for developing and managing these processes:

> Our strategic planning process is the SPaR [strategic planning and review] . . . it really focuses on a three-year horizon in terms of strategic planning and it's the formal strategic planning process. In addition we have a slightly different process, which is more of a once or twice a year survey about five- to seven-year opportunities—I call it the growth review—which is largely about technologies and markets.

In specifically addressing the timelines, Brennan said that "if your planning cycle is 36 months and no longer, then you're missing some things. So I think, we really look at a three-year approach as being the right cycle for our formalized process, and a five- to seven-year approach as being the right cycle for a less formal, more brain-storm-driven approach."

The idea of planning cycles but with built-in flexibility was described by Debra Dunn as needed in the current environment:

> I think the frequency needs to vary, depending on the business. In the way that it used to be, you did three- to five-year strategies and you did them every year. I mean, it was very routinized and for the most part that was OK—you could look out three to five years and pick the big trends and it was OK in most of your businesses. I think it is important now to take a somewhat more agile approach to the process as well and to adjust it depending on what's going on in a particular business.

Commenting from his unique perspective at H-P Labs, Lampman offered additional thoughts on cycles and the need for a less-structured approach: "It's a bit of a messy process. Sometimes we meet with people who have very structured strategy development processes. And my experience is that those tend to work much better in the businesses where the strategy has a shorter time frame."

Responsible for one of H-P's horizontal organizations that directly serves

the H-P businesses and enables them to be more effective, efficient, and informed, Cook commented on her organization's post-merger planning cycle
which seems more improvisational:

> Since both the merger and the changes in the economic environment have
> occurred, our strategic development processes are more ad hoc, and they're
> also more short-term focused than they have been in the past. But at the
> same time, I think they're much more focused on what we can actually do.

Scanning the Environment

An interesting topic that emerged was that if a company is to be agile, it
requires continuous scanning of the external environment. Well-crafted scenarios, which we heard mentioned by several participants, also involve the
definition and tracking of triggers—the explicit attention to environmental
signals, indicating the occurrence of key actions or events. The scanning
requirement is always needed in business, but in the current dynamic environment, it was seen as de rigueur by Debra Dunn:

> So we're on a standard annual cycle, but the way it gets adjusted is: when
> there is a disruption in a particular business, then there's a whole extra set
> of strategic work, thought, dialogue, and analysis that goes on. And that
> can be prompted by a variety of things. It can be prompted by consolida-
> tion in the industry and merger and acquisition issues and opportunities
> that pop up. So, there is sort of the standard process, and underneath it
> there is the "as needed" process that augments it. . . . I think that's the way
> the frequency gets adjusted.

At the enterprise business level, Chaffin commented similarly about her
organization's constant focus on the external signals: "Whoever is leading
the overall business has a good group of people on the staff . . . who constantly read the environment. Literally, the first thing you do every day is, get
online, see what's happened, what's happening today, who announced what."
Even with a well-developed strategy, continually watching the environment
is emphasized by Lampman, H-P Labs: "[E]ven if you have a really good
strategy process for your business, you have a pretty high risk of getting run
over, because the low-level signals, the disruptors, and the indications of
discontinuity sometimes are not very loud."

Scanning the environment was referred to as "reading the weather reports" by several leaders. We heard it from Roger Archibald, who relies on
external networks to effectively scan and plan:

When you are in a market that is developing or moving quickly, it can be beneficial to periodically check in with your peers at other companies. I call this getting weather reports. A new market or a fast-developing market is much like a hurricane—it is hard to predict where it might move next. The more that we can share "weather reports" with others in the industry, the better chance we all have of staying close to the eye of the hurricane.

Conclusions

At the time of the investigation, the environmental conditions were driven by an unstable economic environment in which the company leaders maintained a watchful eye on several major forces: technology innovation, major global competitor moves, corporate scandals, and geopolitical unrest. A juggling act was required that monitored the external signals, maintained current product positions and market share, applied resources to innovation, and managed the largest corporate integration ever witnessed.

With all the change in the global environment, what key strategies were employed at H-P at the time of the investigation? Fifteen months after the acquisition of Compaq was announced and seven months after the deal was closed, Barb Braun, Merger Integration Office, described the following overarching strategic decision, namely, the acquisition of Compaq:

> So I think the strategic issues that H-P is solving by buying Compaq Corporation is to position itself in basically all of its markets to be the number one or number two player. The purpose for the Hewlett-Packard and Compaq get-together was to really bind the best of both companies to create a new company that would be more competitive than either company standing alone. Therefore, the strategy aimed at being number 1 or number 2 in key markets drove the acquisition decision.

Once the acquisition was announced, a plan to efficiently integrate Compaq was engaged at the corporate level with resources specifically allocated to the integration. In the meantime, business units still had to "keep the plane flying" but without a common planning process. It appeared that most pre-merger H-P businesses relied on their tried and true approaches, steeped in ten-step planning, defining objectives, meeting milestones, selling products, maintaining revenue and market share, all while participating in the redesign of the company and integrating new products and 60,000 employees.

Many H-P leaders focused on the need for a less formulaic approach— one that is iterative, involving ad hoc strategic conversation between internal thought leaders, customers, partners—while concurrently reading the weather reports. It appeared, however, that most who spoke about an organized strategy formulation and planning approach were speaking with an ideal future state perspective, namely, once the integration period reached a point of resolution. Even if the end of the merger integration period was their common reference point, strategic management was discussed as a deliberate approach, namely, determining a strategic direction based on customer and market conditions. Although most believed that it would serve as a foundation for strategy formulation, it would need to be flexible enough to change as environmental forces impacted the corporation.

Due to the uniqueness of the investigation period—a tumultuous environment along with the added corporate integration—strategic management for H-P leaders was more demanding than without a merger to manage. A similar study with fewer internal dynamics might well yield different leader perspectives on the role of strategic management. However the question is, will such conditions ever exist again?

— 3 —

Thinking Strategically in Los Angeles County

Incorporated in 1850, Los Angeles County, with approximately 9.8 million people, is the most populous county in the nation, exceeded only by eight states.[1] The County encompasses an area of nearly 4,100 square miles, consisting of 88 cities and significant unincorporated areas. Its $339 billion economy would rank it sixteenth among the world's countries. Not surprisingly, its over $17 billion annual budget would rank the County as a Fortune 200 company by revenue, exceeding such varied corporate giants as Coca-Cola Enterprises, Xerox, 3M, Duke Energy, and Wellpoint Health Networks.

Los Angeles County is considered by many to be the milieu for nearly all social and political issues within the United States. These include debates over how to manage the enormous immigrant inflow, integrate the diversity of populations (over 60 languages are spoken), stem a hemorrhaging health care system, lessen ethnic tensions and gang violence, reduce economic disparities, and attract a new business base. Among the facts highlighting the demands on County services in 2002–2003 were 3 million outpatient health visits and 302,000 emergency room visits, MediCal eligibility benefits for 1.62 million persons per month, and counseling, mediation, and investigative help for 700,000 consumer affairs persons.

Los Angeles County operates under a charter form of government, originally approved in 1912. A five-person, elected Board of Supervisors (chosen by district, each consisting of approximately 2 million people) serves as both the executive and legislative body for the County, enacting ordinances and establishing policies for the administration of the County's departments, commissions, and special districts. Once elected, it is rare for supervisors to lose successive reelections, thereby making them among the most powerful politicians in the nation. The Board of Supervisors oversees a formal organization consisting of 37 departments and 93,000 employees that can be categorized as public protection, human services, recreation and cultural services, general government services, and central support services. The chief administrative officer (and his department) takes a lead role in managing the financial stability and overseeing the implementation of the Board's decisions.

Until the late 1990s these departments operated independently with little coordination across boundaries. In 1998, under the guidance of the chief administrative officer (CAO), the County began a formal strategic planning process that was in its fifth year at the time of this study. The plan identifies both organizational goals (e.g., workforce development) and programmatic goals (children and families) that require multiple departments to work together to develop program outcomes, strategies, and success metrics. For instance, 22 departments are involved collectively, along with many community advocacy groups, to improve the well-being of children and families in five areas: good health, economic well-being, safety and survival, social and emotional well-being, and educational/workforce readiness. For the first time there appears to be a *sense of oneness* at the senior levels, although the widespread internalization among the workforce at lower department levels still seems elusive.

The Interview Sample

Our sample consisted of the chief administrative officer, the assistant chief administrative officer, the section head, in the Chief Administration office, responsible for strategy coordination, the undersheriff, and nine department heads. Table 3.1 provides some basic information for each.

At the time of the study, the County was experiencing a dramatic budget shift. From 1996 to 2001 an overall economic boom had allowed departments to expand resident services. The budget had increased from approximately $12.8 billion to $17.1 billion. It was in this environment that strategic planning had been started. The onset of a major recession in 2001 and the subsequent decrease in revenues had begun to impinge on nonmandated programs and services. Additionally, the health system lost a major federal waiver to receive significant funding, causing a massive health care deficit. This resulted in clinic closings and a reduction in services. Many questioned the ability to sustain the strategic planning directions during the forthcoming years.

Environmental Forces

As shown in Table 3.2, interviewees mentioned 9 different forces (seven external and 2 internal) affecting their departments, a similar number to both

Table 3.1

Interview Sample

Department	Category	Budget (millions)	Employees	Name
Chief Administrative Office	Central Support	$70,954	441	David Janssen/Lari Sheehan/ Martin Zimmerman
Auditor-Controller	Central Support	52,731	446	Tyler McCauley
Fire	Public Protection	601,964	4,002	Michael Freeman
Human Resources	Administrative	37,297	250	Michael Henry
Internal Services	Administrative	373,936	2,485	Joan Ouderkirk
Mental Health	Human Services	1,043,409	2,802	Marv Southard
Parks and Recreation	Recreation & Cultural	99,681	1,276	Tim Gallagher
Probation	Public Protection	514,777	5,145	Richard Shumsky
Public Works	General Government	1,306,227	3,984	Jim Noyes
Community & Senior Services	Human Services	184,276	558	Robert Ryans
Sheriff	Public Protection	1,669,161	15,825	Bill Stonich

Table 3.2

Environmental Forces

External	**Internal**
• Demographics	• Board of Supervisors
• Economy	• Competing departmental needs
• Federal/state rules and regulations	
• Technology	
• Customer demands	
• Homeland security	
• Media	

Hewlett-Packard and the California State University system. Not surprisingly, both the prevailing economic conditions and its potential impact of department budgets and the demographic challenges of an increasingly diverse, needy population dominated the landscape.

Demographics

Two of this book's coauthors (Alan Glassman and Deone Zell) are long-term residents of Los Angeles County and have continually read and heard stories regarding the crushing demand for government services. Yet, the numbers surprised both. Commenting on the number of people receiving assistance from the Department of Public Social Services, for instance, Joan Ouderkirk, director of the Internal Services Department, explained:

> We just had a management conference last week and the welfare director indicated that 20 percent of the residents of Los Angeles County are receiving some kind of assistance from DPSS [the Department of Public Social Services]. That's 20 percent—two million people! That's huge! And, when you add in the uninsured or underinsured, the number gets bigger.

Newspaper articles often express dismay over the inability of programs to impact the nearly 1 million children that are underfed each day.

Elaborating on the challenge to meet the needs of the poor, Tyler McCauley, the auditor-controller, noted the steady influx of immigrants who end up in the County and both the lack of support from the federal government or concern from other states:

> The Feds refuse to acknowledge that there's a problem. And, because most immigrants end up in California, Florida, and New York, the other states

don't care. But, we have to care, because they are here . . . we just have to figure out how to take care of them.

McCauley also noted that many small businesses do not provide sufficient health care, so even employed workers frequently utilize County health facilities, "so you figure the County government is subsidizing a lot of businesses." Commenting specifically on the challenges facing health care system, Michael Henry, the director of Personnel stated:

> Our system is totally designed for putting ill people in hospital beds; we have more hospital beds, I think, than any other county in the country. A lot of money was spent building this system and it takes a lot to keep it going. Yet the federal government has shifted its funding to out-patient, preventive care. So our revenue stream is shrinking, while we continue to have this huge, costly health system.

Henry further noted that the many of Los Angeles' poor as well as certain ethnic groups tended to avoid health care until they were truly in poor health, making it almost impossible for the County to shift to preventive care as quickly as the federal government wanted. Henry expected a $350 million budget shortfall for the department, the closing of hospitals, and layoffs among the 20,000 Department of Health employees.

Similarly, at the Department of Mental Health, the number of mentally ill and uninsured poor has grown dramatically. According to Marv Southard, the director of the Department of Mental Health:

> We have in L.A. County a huge problem with serious and persistently mentally ill people who don't have any benefits and still need care. . . . We just did an assessment of uninsured people in treatment at County directly operated clinics and we found a 37 percent increase in the uninsured population that we treat in clinics compared to the same four-month period last year.

Southard, like many department heads, expects the situation to worsen due to spillover from other social sector agencies that are suffering budget difficulties and thereby referring clients to the County:

> As the economy continues to go down, and MediCal (Medicaid) curtailments have made eligibility harder, more and more people wind up on the street. This makes visible the seriously and persistently mentally ill on the streets, often with substance abuse problems. I think that's a danger for us, since people ask, What's our mental health system doing? Look at all those people. Why can't we help them?

Southard points out that language barriers compound the challenge, highlighting the difficulties of addressing mental illness in the Hispanic community:

> One of the things that hasn't happened is the full recognition of our undertreatment of Spanish-speaking persons with mental illness. If you look at the difference between our treatment population and our MediCal population, for example, we provide more treatment to every other population. . . . That's primarily a factor of not enough Spanish-speaking mental health professionals.

According to the chief administrative officer, David Janssen, "language is a huge issue for all our programs that provide services; for example, the changing ethnic makeup of the County means ballots have to be printed in seven languages."

The interrelated pressures brought about by the persistent social service and health needs of the residents are exacerbated by the demands of an increasingly aging population. According to Robert Ryans, director of the Department of Community and Senior Services:

> The demographic clock doesn't stop, aging doesn't stop because you have a budget problem. The long-term care issue is driving a lot of us in terms of the type of County we want to see in three or five or seven years. How can we collaborate to make that a more positive situation?

At the other end of the spectrum, Richard Shumsky, the chief probation officer, talked about both the influx of high-risk youth and the increase in violent gang activity. He worried that a very visible campaign to crack down on gangs by the City of Los Angeles's new chief of police and the County sheriff would hinder some of his department's most successful community-based efforts with youthful offenders:

> [Y]ou have to shift some directions to align yourself with law enforcement. And we can be overwhelmed because if law enforcement is more proactive, then no matter what we plan, our detentions will skyrocket. We will have to shift resources to detention.

Finally, the demographics of the County present an internal workforce challenge. Jim Noyes, director of the Department of Public Works, identified the difficulty in hiring minority engineers, noting that "you don't have a lot of minorities going to engineering school." Ouderkirk was troubled by the exodus of the baby-boomers and the loss of institutional knowledge, and Henry worried about the inability of government to compete for talent in today's marketplace.

The Economy

Perhaps the most incessant concern of the County leadership was not having the funding to meet the identified needs of their clients. Many seemed genuinely "pained" as they described the consequences of the current economic slump to their clientele, yet these leaders simultaneously accepted the cyclical nature of the economy and its impact on their operations. At the time of the study, the legislature was confronting a $35 billion budget shortfall, necessitating a reduction in funds to municipalities. Unlike the private sector or federal government, state and local municipalities have to balance their budgets each year. According to CAO Janssen, "we had four good years, now we're going back into a very bad, very hard crisis—everybody is going to be impacted." Similarly, Bill Stonich, the undersheriff, seemed to capture the prevailing view:

> The most pressing on-going issue for law enforcement administrators is the lack of a stable funding source. My experience throughout my 37-year career as a law enforcement officer and law enforcement executive can be simply described as a roller coaster of funding and lack of funding. Our current budget crisis has been repeated every six to eight years for as long as I can remember.

The difficulties were exacerbated both by the inability to raise property taxes substantially to "make up" any of the local shortfall (due to the passage of a state constitutional initiative in 1978) and the state's withholding of federal block funding and general fund revenues, so that the funds could be applied toward balancing the state's budget. An account by Michael Freeman, the fire chief, captured the dilemma:

> At first, the federal government distributed terrorism grants to the 157 largest jurisdictions in the United States, including both the City of Los Angeles and the County of Los Angeles. The grant money came directly to the County. Once the County received the funding, it would be passed to the Office of Emergency Management where it would be apportioned to accommodate the various needs identified within the County. For several years, the funds were split 50-50 between the Sheriff's Department and the Fire Department. About two years ago, the federal government made a decision, I think with input from the governors, to send future money via the state channel. The states would be entitled to 25 percent of that grant money and 75 percent would be allocated to local government, through the state. And, we're still waiting to see that money, about $20 million, come through the state. Even more significant to local govern-

ment is the $3.5 billion that the Bush administration has earmarked for Homeland Security.

Both Freeman and Jim Noyes, director of the Department of Public Works, received special district funding, which further increased their risk. According to Noyes:

> The governor made some proposals to balance the state budget by taking about $500,000 from funds sitting around in cities' and counties' housing development projects. Those people screamed bloody murder about it. Well, we have all kinds of pots of money in our special districts, where such a raid is fathomable. Who knows!

Noyes believed that his department was somewhat protected by the ability of the Board of Supervisors to raise rates without voter approval, thereby mitigating any "raid by the state." On the other hand, Freeman noted that his department's growth was dependent on the small yearly increases in property taxes and that in difficult times, he would be in competition with other departments for additional funding.

For the few departments that received nearly all their funding from the state general fund, the impact of the budget crisis was potentially disastrous. As explained by Tim Gallagher, director of the Department of Parks and Recreation:

> Our issue is strictly money. We're looking at a $35 million cut out of $63 million in general fund support, so it is major. If we lose $35 million, it's beyond devastation. We'll be a system of golf courses and nothing else.

Noting that Parks and Recreation could attempt to compete for more county property tax money, Gallagher was realistic:

> We don't compete well against fire and police. We don't do a good job in arguing our impact to the community as well as fire and police, and quite frankly, we don't have the scare tactic that they have.

At the other end of the spectrum, Department of Community and Senior Services director Ryans noted that his department received nearly 90 percent of its budget from federal or state offsets, and therefore these funds were not likely to be reduced.

As the County leaders focused on the ramifications of the economic crisis on their ability to provide services, several commented on the sustainability of the strategic planning process, which had begun during an economic upswing. While several wondered about possible negative competition between departments, CAO Janssen presented an optimistic view:

> Our message to the departments is: This is when you really need the strategic planning effort, more than when times are good, and we are continuing. Frankly, I don't think we have lost any momentum yet on behalf of the departments, but the budget will increasingly be a challenge to our effort to continue.

The assistant CAO, Lari Sheehan, put forth a similar assessment, stating that "the challenge is to accept that the strategic planning effort will help us get through this downturn. And, I think we're very successful at it right now."

Federal/State Rules and Regulations

The public sector represents "an industry" with an intricate set of interdependencies both within and between structural levels. For instance, states and municipalities cannot refuse to implement federal laws and regulations even when they are promulgated without sufficient funds or withhold services from those who qualify, even when offering the service results in disproportionate expenditures. Similarly, states can impose new regulations or require additional reporting of data from municipalities without any additional allocation of resources. For Los Angeles County, this presents an ongoing challenge. For example, the passage of welfare reform required the Department of Public Social Services to undertake a three-year restructuring that necessitated the retraining of nearly every social worker and the design and implementation of a new record keeping system at County cost. As summarized by Sheehan:

> We are agents of the state and federal government. They expect us to administer their programs, and yet they want to tie our hands about how we go about doing that. And, if we don't follow their rules, they penalize us.

From our interviewees, two examples provided by Fire Chief Freeman highlight the impact of "simple" compliance in the nation's largest municipality:

> Four years ago, the state determined that whenever firefighters had to enter a smoky atmosphere that was potentially life-threatening and dangerous, they had to do so in pairs. In addition to the initial attack crew of the pair of firefighters, there also had to be an external crew of two firefighters—this is commonly referred to as "two in and two out." This requirement has

called for us to send one additional unit to every structure fire . . . it makes sense, but it's had a significant impact on us.

In addition to the two in, two out rule, a few years ago the state passed a law that required individual fitting of the breathing apparatus face piece for every firefighter. For about 3,000 firefighters, we conducted fit tests where technicians had to test different-size face pieces on each firefighter to establish the right fit.

Several County leaders grumbled about the insensitivity of lawmakers to the realities of day-to-day governance, even when the purposes of new regulations were viewed favorably. Noyes, of Public Works, for instance, stated:

We have more and more rules with respect to workers' compensation and more and more protection of employees. This is all good! But more and more, these rules coming out of higher-level government organizations are impacting our resources—they require more involvement on our part. Auditing requirements and financial requirements are becoming more and more common, much more so than they used to be.

Similarly, he noted that new water quality requirements would cost the County $69 million—"a lot of money."

Reflecting on these ever-increasing requirements imposed on municipalities, assistant CAO Sheehan mused:

I always thought it would be a really good idea to take all the employees who worked for Congress, the federal and state agencies, and the state legislature and have them take a two-year sabbatical. They would have to work for a local government agency or even a private company that had to deal with the regulations that they were writing—I don't think they have a real understanding of the impact on municipalities. I mean, it's one thing to hold hearings around the state and pass new requirements; it's another thing to make these things work and figure out how to finance them.

Technology—Customer Demand

Several years ago, Mark Saladino, the treasurer-tax collector for Los Angeles County, told the following story to one of Alan Glassman's classes:

Shortly after I assumed my position, I received a call from one of the members of the Board of Supervisors. I was asked a very simple question: Why did a person who lived over 75 miles from downtown and needed an official copy of a parcel tax record need to (a) take a day off from work to drive downtown, (b) pay $20 to park, and (c) wait in line for over two hours? The supervisor's question reflected an increasing number of citizen complaints about the whole world being able to transact business on-line, why not the County. Soon, I was receiving similar queries from other supervisors. I knew that my operation had to start adopting new technologies—immediately. At the same time, the financial constraints seemed overwhelming.

This reflected a common pressure for government—citizens are increasingly viewing themselves as customers, demanding that government provide services equal to those offered by the private sector. Auditor-Controller McCauley summarized:

> The public expects that if they can go up to a teller machine, they can get cash immediately. They can pay their insurance bills over the Internet and they can have checks deposited directly into their bank accounts. So when dealing with the County, they want to be able to pay their property taxes over the Internet.

McCauley also noted that the County was committed to more involvement by the public. In fact, at the time of this study, nearly all departments in the County were engaged in customer satisfaction studies and most were considering the use of technology as the primary tool for increasing program responsiveness.

Yet implementing large technological projects is extremely difficult, given the high public-sector costs of installing these services. This creates a clash between long-term technological needs and immediacies. As explained by CAO Janssen:

> The County is probably doing an okay job on technology. Like most government agencies, we do small projects just fine; we don't, however, do large technology projects particularly well. And, almost all of our projects, because of the size of our client pool, are very large. . . . You know, we're looking at putting in an Enterprise Resource Process (ERP) in the County, about $100 million and maybe a 50-50 chance of success—not because of the software, but because of the difficulties of implementation. And, of course, this is coming at the same time that we are talking about closing hospitals. So, how do you convince the Board to invest in a financial data system at a time when you are closing hospitals? You know, it's virtually impossible.
>
> The County has everything from the Sheriff's Department to Children's Services to the County Registrar. We may have reached our capacity for reacting to change in terms of responding to information technology. We're not like on TV, where everything happens fast. People don't understand that. Our adaptive capacity is simply slow, which the public doesn't understand. It takes time to get there.

It was clear that the leaders wanted to do more and were discouraged by their inability to fund technology projects. As stated by Internal Services' Ouderkirk, "We're not taking nearly as much advantage of the capabilities of technology that we could. It is very difficult in the public sector to invest in the future when survival in the present is always a financial struggle." Similarly, Noyes from Public Works stated that "we've got to use—more and more—the Internet and tools of e-commerce that are available and much more prevalent in the private sector." Parks and Recreation's Gallagher was more explicit:

> [A]t the Department of Parks and Recreation, all reservations are still done by hand, and the department is not yet integrated into the County Internet system. Imagine, if I take my laptop home, I can talk to the other County folks, but I can't talk to my own department.

At the same time, some department heads were quite pleased with the technology they had been able to adopt. According to Fire Chief Freeman, "We certainly use computer modeling to help us with fire station locations and, of course, we use the computer to help us dispatch equipment." Commenting on engineering projects within his department, Noyes asserted:

> Its changed tremendously. . . . When I look at what our engineers are doing today with respect to the engineering aspects of the job, compared to the way it was done when I first entered the workforce, and even when I was doing work 15 or 20 years ago, it is tremendously different due to technology and the ability to use computers and other technological tools.

As we listened to these leaders, it became apparent that they were engaged in a continuous balancing act. On one side of the equation was both the public demand that the County match the private sector's technological advances and their personal desire to improve service delivery through technology applications. On the other side of the equation was both the recognition of the high cost, long development/implementation time frame for adoption of new technology and an acceptance that "politicians" needed to apply funds to critical immediacies. It seemed to be an enormously difficult course to chart.

Homeland Security

Preparedness for domestic terrorism as a new force in America's geopolitical decision-making and the concomitant requirements of local municipalities for homeland security began to emerge during the early stages of our study. According to Fire Chief Freeman:

It is still somewhat unknown, and it has many facets to it. One facet is the department trying to stay current with technology; another is us trying to coordinate with all three levels of government: local, state, federal. There's a lot of funding that comes from the federal government down through the states to local government.

When it comes to terrorism preparedness, there are implications that involve equipment and personnel training. It brings up strategic issues in terms of how to redirect staff to take on the management of the additional responsibilities. There is the "ongoing drilling," as we call it, that involves the practice and the exercises. The exercises include countywide coordination that involves many departments. I really cannot emphasize enough how the terrorism issue has affected the fire service and our department.

Both Freeman and Ryans from Community and Senior Services also noted the immense health-related challenges, including the limited number of trauma centers to handle victims, the need to train first-responders in hazardous materials disposal and decontamination procedures, and the impact of resource reallocations on all departments.

Media

A common theme among public-sector officials, regardless of the level of government, is their on-going "clash" with the media. Public officials believe that the media are interested only in negative stories—positive stories do not attract readers and/or viewers. CAO Janssen summarized:

I've been dealing with the media since 1977. They clearly haven't become any more supportive of government, and probably more destructive to the political system. Nobody in their right mind would run for government in this country, because as soon as you put your name forth they're going to start ripping you apart; it doesn't matter who you are, Republican, Democrat or Independent. They want perfect people to run for office. And, if there were perfect people, the last place you'd want them is in government, because you do not want perfect people running the government.

In any event, the media are extraordinarily destructive. They obviously don't report good things, they only report the bad, and their information systems and communications are so intrusive that a single bad event is transmitted instantaneously throughout the world; you do a few bad events in a week, and people believe that everything is bad, when in fact, I think, if you look at almost any program, whether it's welfare or almost anything, one out of ten is what you are dealing with, which means that nine out of ten are just fine. You never read about the nine out of ten!

Similarly, Auditor-Controller McCauley complained: "We constantly get criticized by the newspapers . . . who love to chop up government" and "it is the bad news for the most part, nobody wants to hear the good things." He offered the following example:

> Someone told the press that we lose 1 percent of all foster care children. There are 40,000 children in the system, and 400 of them are missing. Of those, we probably know that 85 percent were stolen by their parents and have crossed the state line. But the perception created is that we cannot keep track of the children and the public is horrified . . . so that drives government. The press is a huge influence on the government, huge.

McCauley did add, however, that the media can provide appropriate pressure to improve, he just wants better balance.

Board of Supervisors—Competing Departmental Needs

Members of the Board of Supervisors, as elected public officials, operate within a political framework. Thus, multiple, very diverse constituencies influence decision-making, and day-to-day immediacies tend to dominate public comments. This creates a natural tension between department heads, career civil servants, and the Board. Moreover, since the Board holds regularly scheduled public meetings on most Tuesdays to discuss County business, decide issues, and allocate funds, department leaders are drawn into the political arena. As depicted by HR's Henry, this makes it very difficult for the Board to tolerate mistakes by department heads and "prevents people from stepping out and taking a risk." Henry further explained that an important role for department heads is to buffer your people from the politics, noting, "a good department head will take the hit, act as a buffer." Gallagher stated that it is imperative for a department head to keep the respect of the Board, since there is always a competition for resources.

Ouderkirk from Internal Services noted that due to political considerations, it is more difficult to do strategic planning in the public arena than in business, but asserted, "I think it can be done." She explained:

> In my experience Board office staff do not generally have the time nor inclination to get involved in strategic planning at the detailed programmatic level. I also do not think that they need to be involved in the details—that is what they pay us for, to run the organization effectively. The challenge at the

County level is maintaining the commitment necessary to keep the bureaucracy focused on furthering strategic agendas in the face of competing political issues. I do believe that we can be responsive to important political issues and also move the County toward important strategic objectives.

CAO Janssen offered a detailed elaboration on the difficulty of conducting strategic planning in a political context:

It is political first of all, although we are extraordinarily fortunate that we have a stable Board. There is nothing more dysfunctional to government than having a constant change of public officials and you can see that everywhere; you can see it in Sacramento with term limits. This particular Board has been together now for eight years, and there's a very good likelihood that these five will be around for another six years. That is hugely important to an organization because public officials can do very good and they can do very bad. . . . [T]hat's an advantage of the political environment we have in LA, we really have an opportunity to do significant changes.

Strategic planning in government can almost be an oxymoron, because most governments have turnover every four years, in Congress every two years. Well, when you have to get reelected every two or four years, you are event driven by necessity. You know, you just don't plan for the future. For one thing, it's not particularly rewarding to people because they want their potholes fixed, they don't want to see a strategic plan. And so you're focused on doing the potholes. So planning in government is very, very difficult. . . . You shouldn't just have a strategic plan that says "in five years, I'm going to do something," and you work on it for five years and then you start over again. You've got to have shorter-range goals, politically as well, so the elected officials clearly see you accomplishing something; they're not going to stand by for a plan that's going to take five years, they're not going to be here in five years.

How can we engage in a strategic plan effort when the Board members every Tuesday have fifty thousand things for us to do? Well, you have to do both. You know, we can multitask, we have brains, we're intelligent people—we'll just do both. We'll do event planning and we'll do strategic planning at the same time. And, technology, you know, will eventually make it easier to do.

The Circle Game

In her classic folk song, "The Circle Game," composer/singer Joni Mitchell begins each of the four verses by describing a child's explorations and dreams at the different phases of youth. At the conclusion of each of these verses, the chorus reminds us that the process of maturation has predictability to it and that "we're captive on a carousel of time." As we listened to many of our interviewees, a distinct, repetitive "story line" seemed to emerge: (1) the economic forces and the pace of change have created a difficult time; (2) we have been through similar times before, we have much institutional knowledge, and we will muddle through; (3) unlike the private sector, overall survival is never an issue; and (4) times will get better and the cycle will begin again. For example, speaking about the resiliency of government, Shumsky from Probation stated:

> [C]oming from government work, we think that we're in it for the long haul. So it's not like private industry. . . . We just know there will be better times. I think the answer is because we've seen it before.

Both Shumsky and Ryans noted that CAO Janssen had told department heads that "we know how to manage crisis, so we simply have to get back to doing it." Indeed, Ryans suggested that government actually does its best work under trying circumstances. For us, Janssen said it best when he wryly predicted that "the County of L.A. will be here in fifty years, so we don't have a problem."

Similarly, the increasing pace of change did not unsettle these leaders. It seemed that the combination of longevity of government service, repetition of circumstances, and the constant need to respond to elected officials alleviated much of the potential stress. As summarized by Martin Zimmerman, manager in the CAO's office:

> I've been in this office for 18 years, so I know the demands. I would not say that the demands are substantially greater now than before. The demands on this office have always been extraordinary and its always been that way. I really don't recall there being a more easily paced time. It has always been you know, snap to, scramble, hustle!

Elaborating on this perspective, HR's Henry posits on the ability of people to adapt to change:

> Back in the late '80s and '90s, we talked about the pace of change and it was described as a tidal wave. Well, we're on that wave now and I don't as a manager see the pace of change being much faster than it was for me nine or ten years ago when I became a department head. I've gotten use to being on the "white-water rapids," if you will, and it just doesn't seem much faster to me.
> For those of us who have been here a long time, it doesn't feel any different. . . . I think we're living change and we have recalibrated our-

selves—it just doesn't feel fast. Or, to say it differently, if this makes sense, it feels fast, but it feels normal.

Strategic Planning in Los Angeles County

In assessing public-sector strategic planning, Glassman and Winograd (2004) note that "only minimal success has been reported" and that "government officials often express 'pain' when discussing their experiences with strategic planning." The authors speculate that this can be attributed, in part, to the adoption of private-sector approaches that fail to account for the inherent contextual differences between the sectors:

> In the private sector, the planning emphasis is on accelerating strategic decision making as a means for attaining competitive advantage. In government, however, agencies must spend significant time seeking agreement from a wide range of stakeholders before a decision is implemented . . . stakeholders who expect to have input.
>
> In addition, the most powerful constituents often decide the budgets and rules for judging performance—and those decisions can be in conflict with the desire of the agency's leaders. Then, there are the media and NGOs[2] . . . that have very narrow interests, but they are very visible and can create a distorted picture of an agency's performance. (p. 331)

The authors assert that because of the number of active stakeholders, strategic planning in the public sector is more complex and needs to become more inclusive and more disciplined than in the private sector.

Setting the Foundation for Strategic Planning (1994–1997)

During the mid-1990s, Los Angeles County confronted a severe fiscal crisis. As the situation worsened, members of the Board of Supervisors recognized that the business of government had to be done differently. Below are several comments by Board members, taken from the public record:

- Counties are caught in a vise between mandates and limited resources (1994).
- We need to provide a blueprint for the future and a vision of how County services will be provided with the available resources (1994).
- The time has come to move beyond crisis management to strategic, long-term planning (1995).
- These are tough times for government, especially counties. . . . To do its job, County government is going to have to change (1995).
- Given that increased demand on County services continues at unprecedented

rates, the Board must begin to look beyond one fiscal year in its budgeting process in order to provide better planning, develop strategies to downsize, and better anticipate expenditures over a multiyear period (1995).

As a consensus emerged to more effectively manage resources, the Board took two significant actions toward the end of 1995:

1. Established a Blue Ribbon Budget Task Force—consisting of prominent business, educational, and civic leaders—to (a) develop a more effective approach to service delivery, (b) more effectively downsize County government without devastating services, and (c) better anticipate revenues and cultivate more stable sources of revenues to fund ongoing services.
2. Proposed Vision 2000, the development of a four-year strategic plan "to provide a thoughtful opportunity for County rightsizing, rather than across-the-board cuts or one-time cuts for quick fix solutions." Included in the guidelines on how to proceed was the instruction that every department head establish a strategic plan centered on their core missions and critical services.

The Blue Ribbon Budget Task Force proposed several ideas for consolidation; its most significant impact, however, was a set of recommendations around strategic planning, an area that was not part of the original charge. In its investigation of department operational practices, the Task Force concluded that there was virtually no alignment of planning within County departments, there were insufficient linkages between planning, budgeting, and cost control centers, and there were inadequate interactions between departments within the same service area. As a consequence, in May 1996, the Board instructed the chief administrative officer to take the following actions:

• Develop a Countywide Strategic Plan to be implemented in fiscal year 1997/98; the plan was to reflect Countywide priorities for the next three–five years.
• Establish cluster-level (e.g., public safety, health) strategic planning to identify systems issues and develop strategic initiatives and necessary action plans.
• Develop a process for allocating resources to these strategic initiatives on a multiyear basis.

These mandates were incorporated into Vision 2000 and the CAO developed a set of reporting procedures to track progress on the development and implementation of department strategic plans.

This initial effort at strategic planning was basically unsuccessful! First, and to be expected, because County leaders and CAO staff had only minimal familiarity with strategic planning, their procedures "mimicked" conventional planning methods. That is, the planning process at all levels (1) became overly formalized with "hard" deadline dates for delivery of plans and progress reports (every quarter), (2) often adopted an approach that combined unit plans rather than department-wide assessments, and (3) avoided linkages to resource realities. Overall, it represented what Mintzberg (1994a) described as a calculating style rather than the committing style needed for effective strategic planning and what Bryson (2004) cautioned against—the attention to form over-strategic thinking.

Second, the CAO at the time did not believe strongly in strategic planning. Consequently, as department strategic plans were formulated and forwarded to the CAO, no effort was made to (1) synthesize or develop a single County plan, (2) change the criteria for evaluating departments, and (3) allocate resources based on the strategic choices. For most, it became another paper exercise. Then, somewhat surprisingly, the CAO resigned. As the Board began the search for a new CAO, accompanied by the normal rotation of Board leadership, Vision 2000 faded as a "front-burner" issue.

Third, the County departments operated individually, a typical silo-designed government organization. Thus, when strategic planning began, departments adopted different approaches—who should oversee the formulation stage, who should participate in the development, and what internal and external information needed to be gathered. Moreover, language usage differences (e.g., goal, objective, strategy) existed between departments and, on occasion, even within departments. While cluster plans had been encouraged, none emerged. Auditor-Controller McCauley seemed to capture much of the sentiment among long-term County leaders:

> The County didn't use to plan at all. Things would "hit it" and each department would deal with it—it wasn't strategic, it was very decentralized, and we never knew if anyone cared about the direction we followed. We did what we thought was best for our department. . . . So the silos went up.

Ouderkirk from Internal Services added:

> I think it was because people didn't take it seriously. They weren't committed to doing it as a fundamental element of how to conduct business. For example, it had nothing or little to do with the budget.

If At First You Don't Succeed, You Get Another Chance (1997–2000)

David Janssen was hired as the chief administrative officer in August 1996 with the understanding that the County needed to form a more collaborative, less competitive environment among departments. As noted by Janssen:

> The Board said to me that they were very concerned about getting County departments to work together. You have 37 departments reporting to five elected officials, and, if no one is talking to each other, it quickly becomes dysfunctional. From my view, there was no glue to the organization. We were really talking about a cultural change.

A story told by Janssen, and now part of the current folklore, exemplified this departmental individuality:

> Within the first six months, we went to a March of Dimes Walk America, an event in which the County is a very heavy participant. Every department had its own separate T-shirt! There was no L.A. County T-shirt; it was the Department of Social Services, it was the District Attorney, it was the Department of Health. They all had different colors, different type shirts, and the whole thing. I thought it was a very good symbolic representation of where Los Angeles County was when I arrived, which is: every department was doing its own thing.

Reiterating Janssen's initial assessment, Sheehan stated:

> One of the reasons that David Janssen was hired was that the County was operating as 37 little fiefdoms, and because there are five county executives, basically nobody was responsible for pulling them together. The Board asked David, "How will you introduce collaboration?" "How are you going to get the Department Heads to work together?" "How do we get to a systematic approach to planning rather than individual department efforts?" Strategic planning is one of the ways!

When Janssen reintroduced the need to do strategic planning, he envisioned it as a mechanism for potentially profound change.

> We entered into strategic planning, or at least I did, with somewhat simple or minimum expectations on the one hand, and, on the other hand, with a pretty dramatic intent to change the organization. We needed to shift from an organization that was competitive, entrepreneurial, and silo-based to

one that was collaborative, goal-oriented, and results-focused. People needed to see value in integrating services.

Perhaps Janssen's most important early decision relative to strategic planning was to buffer the formulation process from the day-to-day immediacies, providing department heads with the opportunity to explore the subject, learn from each other, and focus on an envisioned future. Janssen, who was CAO in San Diego County prior to accepting the Los Angeles position, noted, "I learned that it takes 13 years to change the culture of an organization, if you're lucky." Commenting on this "mythical" bifurcation, HR's Henry summarized:

> Mr. Janssen announced, very early on, not only to middle and upper managers, but to the Board of Supervisors, that this is not something that is a one- or two-year process. This is something that is going to be very long term and what we're really trying to do is change the way we do business, to change our County culture—that's something that doesn't happen overnight.
>
> This was much different than previous efforts—it provided time to plan. This took a lot of pressure off the organization in terms of performing. The organization, I think, began to recalibrate itself and to think of this as being a long-term process, rather than our usual Board-to-Board meeting or budget-to-budget mentality. We were able to split our thinking into managing the day-to-day functions to keep the place operating and to meet the needs of our boss, the Board of Supervisors and the carving out time to think strategically as a collective body.

According to McCauley, "it finally allowed us to get together to identify strategic issues and to talk seriously about how we could work collaboratively to solve them."

According to Janssen, the actual beginning was happenstance:

> I had been talking periodically with the department heads about concepts, you know collaboration systems, how to think more about the organizational perspective, nothing specific like strategic planning. And then, we kind of fell into the Anderson School of Management at UCLA, it just happened, we didn't seek them out. They had been talking to one of the Board offices about helping the County and the opportunity arose to get involved with someone without having to go out to bid and reviewing all the "tech ears" to figure out what to do. And they did an excellent job!

As CAO Janssen explained the initial effort, he returned to a constant theme of nearly all our interviewees, the ever-present need to resolve political sensitivities:

> We spent about 1½ years with them, I guess, building the foundation for the plan. We started pretty simple with such questions as: Is there any interest in the executive management of the County to do strategic planning? Do they see any need to make changes in the organization? Are you happy with where you are and what's going on? And, we included Board officers in those sessions, which was very uncomfortable for the departments at the beginning. They didn't feel they could talk if the representatives of elected officials were there. So we had to work through all of those basic personal issues before we could start talking about what we would really like to become, before talking about our future.
>
> We developed out of that, out of those sessions, a vision statement that may or may not be a vision statement—it's too long and too wordy—but we did it and we like it!

In nearly all our interviews, the department heads noted that the real importance of these sessions was the learning about each other and the willingness to express differences and seek common understanding. These sessions resulted in agreement on the vision statement, a set of organizational values and four organizational goals and accompanying strategies (i.e., Service Excellence, Workforce Excellence, Organizational Effectiveness, and Fiscal Responsibility). Again, Janssen's reflections highlighted the continual influence of the Board of Supervisors:

> We had 37 department heads sign a Board letter recommending adoption of the vision statement, our philosophy and values, and the four goals. We had a discussion during one of our sessions about whether we would continue, whether we really wanted to do this, if the Board isn't going to support us. We decided that it was important to do, whether or not the Board supported it, but we also realized that it wouldn't work without Board support. . . . Then, the best of all worlds, they adopted it, I think it was December 1999. And, the Board actually added Respect for Diversity to the philosophy.
>
> Not too long after adoption, the Board added the first program goal, which is Children and Families' Well-Being, to the strategic plan. . . . We started with four organizational goals because I was very reluctant to take on program goals; it's hard to get elected officials to prioritize which program is more important than the other, but they did it themselves and said children and families are more important, for example, than public safety, more important than health care.

Elaboration and Learning (2000–2002)

During the next several years, three major concurrent activities dominated the strategic planning process. First, an assessment by an independent consultant concluded that the implementation of the strategic plan lacked sufficient organization and recommended the formation of a *Guiding Coalition* (GC) to centralize the strategic management process.[3] Formed in March 2000, the GC was chaired by the CAO and comprised of 12 department heads and the 5 chief deputies for the Board of Supervisors who agreed to meet monthly to provide— as stated in the GC Charter—"the leadership required to bring about changes in the County of Los Angeles government that will enable the County to achieve the goals of the strategic plan." The Charter further stated that "the role of the GC is to bring energy, a sense of urgency, unity, and personal commitment to the task of improving the performance of the County's government." According to Auditor-Controller McCauley, the GC acted initially as the "butt-kicker!"

> We established a group called the Guiding Coalition whose job is to insure that we keep pushing, pushing. They're the group that says strategic planning is serious, we're serious, and we're going to keep pushing until everyone understands the importance of working collaboratively. . . . The Guiding Coalition's job is to make sure that department heads remember it day by day, week by week as we press forward.

As the GC matured, it assumed increasing responsibility for the County's strategic direction. Among its initial tasks was the revision of the original strategic plan. As summarized by Zimmerman, manager in the CAO's office:

> The GC conducted a countywide executive strategic planning conference, which included all the department heads and Board chief deputies, where they identified the areas where the strategic plan needed to be expanded. They established new programmatic goals and new strategies for all goal areas. They also developed a proposed mission statement, which had not occurred previously.
> The second conference was to be held in November, 2000 where the work of several cluster groups, which took the work of the initial conference and further refined it, will be reviewed and finalized by all department heads before going to the Board for approval. So it will be a complete revision to the strategic plan.

As the GC began to both puzzle out its role in the implementation of the strategic plan and form cross-functional working teams to accomplish specific strategies and objectives, the traditional formulation-implementation gap common to many public-sector strategic planning efforts began to diminish. As observed by Zimmerman:

> I guess I would just say that the work of the GC has added excitement to the strategic planning process. It does really seem to be gaining credibility

and relevance among the executives. Department heads do seem energized by it, very engaged . . . they see a direct link between the work of the GC and what's important to them and what they need to accomplish to be successful. And at first this was not the case. Either they were totally unaware of it or had no desire to be involved in it or it was considered something frou-frou. While that attitude exists among some, I really have seen it become integrated into County thinking.

Assistant CAO Sheehan concurred, stating that "a good number of department heads have taken ownership of the strategic plan. It's not just the CAO leading—it is definitely a team effort."

Shortly after the second executive strategic planning conference, the GC approved the mission statement and three additional programmatic goals for the areas of community services, health and mental health, and public safety and a substantial expansion of strategies. Immediately thereafter, the GC submitted the revision to the Board of Supervisors where it passed unanimously. This received notable attention throughout the County, thereby expanding the dialogue both within departments and between departments and their community stakeholders.

Second, the strategic planning process cascaded to the department level. At the time the GC was formed, the CAO also asked the 37 departments to develop their own strategic plans. As we listened to the line department heads, the influence of the County's beginning experience and the desire to bolster the County's strategic directions became evident. As stated by Undersheriff Stonich:

> In developing our strategic plan, LASD2 [L.A. Sheriff's Department], we took the early work outlined in the County's strategic plan as a preamble for our efforts. The sheriff wanted to support the CAO and directed that we walk in lockstep with him. As a result, we overlapped Sheriff Baca's vision and CAO David Janssen's vision. Combined, they provided a compass for LASD2.

Public Works' Noyes was even more succinct, asserting "We took our cue, in a certain sense, from the process used by the County."

Perhaps most notable during the early stages of departmental strategic planning activities was the commitment to high involvement by internal and external stakeholders. This seemed to signify the acceptance of a customer service orientation in providing government services, a major emphasis during the initial County strategic planning sessions and many early GC discussions. From our perspective, it was symbolic of the beginning cultural shift from tightly controlled silos to a more transparent organization. Indeed, as Ryans from Community and Senior Services commented on his department's outreach, you could hear his pride in their accomplishment:

In developing our plan, we took advantage of an existing advocacy group, a united senior group that has rallied behind senior issues for the last 30 years. It provided an infrastructure for our work. And what we did was set up a 200-member community roundtable. In addition to the community roundtable, which within a year had met every other month, we had an interdepartmental planning body that held meetings for all of the 18 participating departments. And if that wasn't enough, we created a work group out of both the community roundtable and the interdepartmental planning body, called the Work Group. They worked on developing the plan over a year and a half. We created six committees focused around issues such as housing, transportation, and so forth. We also held community forums around the County to obtain very local input. You name it, we had it!

To build this broad base took about six months. We had to make sure that it truly represented the diversity of our community. And then, from the start, we met with them and solicited their input. Then we created the committees that were so key to the success of it.

Southard from Mental Health described a similar process for external involvement, noting that his department had begun its process prior to the first department head strategic planning meeting:

We began several years ago. . . . We started the process by holding a series of community meetings in which we asked: What services do people with mental health illness deserve? What would the spectrum of service look like, if money was not an issue? You know, what would be the shape of such a system? And we held, I don't know, maybe 40 or 50 community meetings, in which all our stakeholder groups took part.

After the meetings, we found, obviously, that we had way too much information, so we formed a steering group to comb the information for action items that could be tied to outcomes. We probably had 40 of these benchmark goals. Then we did community presentations, prioritized our goals, and established a set of measurements, benchmarks, and outcomes for each goal. That became our Comprehensive Community Care program.

Parks and Recreation's Gallagher, who was new to the County, envisioned a similar outreach process, stating that, "Our intention is to survey our different communities to determine their specific needs—we've identified 30 key stakeholders as a starting point."

Many of these line department heads also shifted toward high internal participation, again breaking with the top-down orientation often heard among employees. The approach by Public Works, as described by Noyes, was akin to similar efforts throughout the County:

We conducted focus groups and, additionally, through a survey, we gave every employee the opportunity to comment on what he or she felt was important to the department. Then the management team worked with the focus group and survey data to really isolate the highest priorities. We had three major half-day or full-day sessions with our division heads and several of their assistants. And the result was a strategic plan that aligned with the County's plan, but also contained elements that highlighted our department's distinctiveness.

As pointed out by Stonich, the Sheriff's Department not only used employees throughout the department, but also publicly committed itself to implementation:

We drew up a team consisting not only of the executive and management branch of the department, but also of a slice of the organization that included deputy sheriffs, professional civilian staff, clerks, etc. who provided input into the exploration of ideas and the development of the plan itself. The team was headed by a division chief and included one commander from each of the 11 divisions within the department. They had permission to go off-site for days at a time to conduct focus groups. Their charge was, "What would the Los Angeles County Sheriff's Department look like, if we didn't know what it looked like?" The team was asked to question everything, even the very role of law enforcement. For a paramilitary organization such as ours, this was unprecedented.

The final plan was not simply a three-ring binder to be copied and placed on a shelf. It was shared with the entire organization, nearly 16,000 people. The sheriff publicly announced the completion of the strategic plan at a well attended press conference. We printed hundreds of copies of LASD2 and distributed them throughout the County family and the community at large. We put ourselves on notice to all that this is what our strategic plan is all about, this is what our organization intends to do, and this is what we believe the Sheriff's Department needs to look like to better serve the people of Los Angeles County into the 21st century.

As we listened to these and other line operational leaders, we became aware of a subtle, yet not unexpected, disconnect between them and the leaders of support departments (e.g., auditor-controller, human resources). Simply stated:

1. Line leaders were passionate when explaining their departmental strategic plans, particularly the widespread involvement of external stakeholders; they seemed to personally relish their connection with large segments of their stakeholder community.

2. Line leaders were highly cognizant of the County's strategic plan and its potential to impact their actions—several described the County plan as a roadmap; some of our line interviewees who served on the Guiding Coalition did not express the same emotional commitment at that level.

3. Support leaders, on the other hand, rarely mentioned their own strategic plans, focusing primarily on the County as a whole; they were excited by the unified actions at the macro level.

Third, in addition to the establishment of the Guiding Coalition and the adoption of strategic planning at the departmental level, the Guiding Coalition decided to address a major divide in government strategic planning—the lack of linkage between budget decisions and strategic plans. As stated by Southard from Mental Health:

In government, to my mind, the budget process ends up happening separate from the strategic planning process. I mean, the two interface incompletely. So, for example, we'll have a central staff budget analyst delete several of our positions or curtail programs as a result of an understanding of what might occur during budget deliberations; however, the analyst never really attempts to understand the outcomes we are trying to achieve. It's simply formula driven!

From our perspective, as a consequence of this dichotomy, the budget becomes the more important issue and the will to implement strategic plans diminishes.

At the time of the interviews, the GC had just undertaken a new program referred to as Performance Counts! (PC!), which established a common framework for collecting and reporting performance information based on program outcomes. As contained in a variety of documents, PC! sought to identify the (1) intended results from the program services or interventions, (2) program indicators to quantify the achievement of those results, that is, the impact on the clients served, and (3) operational measures, such as input/output ratios, efficiency indicators, and customer satisfaction data. In short, PC! focused on two questions: Are we doing the right stuff? Are we doing it the right way?

The introduction of PC! information would be incorporated into the 2004/ 05 budgets, thereby creating the first official link between program outcomes, program costs, and decisions regarding the allocation of resources. It would be accompanied by a major educational effort for department managers and central budget analysts. It was believed that this linkage between planning and budgeting processes would guide future department-level strategic planning updates and, perhaps more important, lead to on-going strategic thinking.

The Role of Leadership

When describing the strategic planning process, several of the interviewees described their role as being the equivalent to a navigator or guide. Fire Chief Freeman stated, for example, "My role is to just be sure that the department's compass setting is accurate, and to champion our efforts," while in Public Works, Noyes envisioned himself as "making sure we stay on track and keeping the Board offices, the CAO, and other affected departments informed as to what we're doing relative to meeting the strategic plan." Gallagher from Parks and Recreation offered a slightly more active role:

> I think my role is to lead this organization and, you know, I see strategic planning no differently than I see day-to-day management. I see myself as the conductor of the orchestra. And my job is not to play any of the instruments; I probably don't even know how to play half of them. My job is to pick the right people for seat number 1, 2, and 3 and make them blend into one unison voice. I also get to pick the type of music we play.

Others noted that they were not well versed in strategic planning when the formulation process began, but quickly accepted the fact that there was no substitute for their personal sponsorship. Many had a similar verse: Our people and our external stakeholders will judge my leadership by my success in implementing the strategic plan.

Halos and Blemishes

The leaders were in relative agreement regarding the benefits they derived from the strategic planning process. As noted above, the most apparent advantage was the focus on alignment. As stated by Ryans from Community and Senior Services:

> If your department plan is not congruent with the County plan, you must ask yourself, why are we doing this? Well, this alignment soon builds down into the branches of the department and the divisions, and so on. It is through this comprehensive alignment that we demonstrate our commitment to collaboration and working together toward solving problems.

Similarly, Public Works' Noyes was about to initiate alignment with the County plan:

One of the major efforts that we're going to undertake, as soon as the Board approves the most recent revision to the County strategic plan, is to take a look at our department plan and make any adjustments to make sure that they mesh.

Shumsky from Probation seemed to say it best when he concluded that "Everybody is aligning themselves with everyone else, and everything has a flow to it. It feels very, very comprehensive."

Others noted the emergence of multiyear thinking and a clear set of priorities, the willingness to engage in constructive disagreements, the commitment to measuring results and sharing performance outcomes with the public, and the sharing of lessons learned among the leadership. Reflecting on these evolving behaviors, HR's Henry summed up:

We are able to think differently. I mean, our thinking before was Tuesday-to-Tuesday, or just fiscal year. Now we are thinking more long-term and we are thinking positively—you know, how are we going to fill this hole in the budget? How are we going to deal with layoffs? How are we going to deal with this program that doesn't work? It's a collective effort and that brings a positive nature, I think, to the organization. It also says that we care about our organization because we are able to talk about these difficult topics constructively.

While the positive aspects of collective planning and action dominated the conversation, these County leaders were also acutely aware of the restrictions and/or challenges to the implementation of their strategic planning efforts. Foremost, as previously noted by Janssen, was the impact of daily events. No one expressed this more ardently than Fire Chief Freeman:

We never know when we're going to have a major emergency incident. For example, this past summer, continuing through January, we just had a very active and demanding fire season. Depending on the size of the fire, it can actually place the department into a skeleton crew situation; everyone is committed to the fire and supporting the personnel on the fire. At such times work can get in the way, and that is one of our major challenges.

In the same way, Noyes asserted that "It's just finding the time to do the in-depth quality work that the working groups and leaders feel needs to be done."

Another barrier to implementation, at both the County and departmental levels, was the difficulty in driving the process beyond the senior management. According to Zimmerman, "A continuing challenge is to drive the plan throughout the organizations; we must find a way to bring everybody on board." Sheehan concurred, providing the following description of the challenge:

> Because of how geographically decentralized the County offices are, people are hired by a department, hired at a specific locations, hired to perform a specific set of tasks. Consequently sometimes, maybe many times, they don't think of themselves as being part of Los Angeles County. They think of themselves, for example, as being social worker X who deals with certain kinds of benefits for children or indigent adults in a certain area. Or, they see themselves as truck driver Y who deals with snow removal in the Antelope Valley. So one of the strategies we're adding is the communications strategy to determine how we can bring the strategic plan to 95,000 employees. How do we communicate with them? How do we get information out to them? How do we bring them in and make them team members?

Ryans worried that until the line employees understood the plan, it would remain, for most, an abstract exercise. He worried about its sustainability, stating, "We really haven't found a way to bring it to the grass roots. . . . I think if David [Janssen] turned to something else tomorrow, it would go away." Beyond the focus on time constraints due to everyday immediacies and the need to drive knowledge and involvement further into the organization, others noted that maintaining Board interest remained problematic, obtaining "good information" for decision-making about programs would take many years, and overcoming the lack of strategic planning knowledge among managers could undermine the effort, despite the promising beginning. In short, we sensed that many believed that although many supporting programs were being put into place, the long-term viability of strategic planning was still shaky.

— 4 —

Thinking Strategically at the California State University

History of the California State University

The largest public education system in the world, the California State University (CSU) consist of 23 campuses spread throughout the Golden State, from San Diego in the south to Humboldt County in the north. The oldest campus—San Jose State University—was founded in 1857 and became the first institution of public higher education in California. The newest campus— California State University, Channel Islands—opened in fall 2002. The campuses of the CSU include comprehensive and polytechnic universities and, since July 1995, the California Maritime Academy, a specialized campus. Considered the "workhorse" of California's system of public education, the CSU offers more than 1,600 bachelor's and master's degrees in over 240 subject areas, and awards more than half the bachelor's degrees and a third of the master's degrees granted in the state. In 2003 the system enrolled more than 400,000 students—twice the number of the University of California (UC) system. Historically the education provided by the CSU has been low cost to ensure access. Tuition to the system is less than the average for any other state in the country, and less than half the average of all four-year public institutions.

While today the universities that comprise the CSU exist as a unified system, they began as a collection of individual "teaching colleges," or training schools for elementary school teachers. In 1960 the Donahoe Higher Education Act brought together the colleges as a system and broadened their function to include undergraduate and graduate instruction in the liberal arts and sciences, in applied fields, and in the professions. The Donahoe Act, also known as the Master Plan, also differentiated the mission of the CSU from the other two public education systems in California—the UC system and the California Community Colleges (CCC). According to the Master Plan, the CSU would be responsible for undergraduate and graduate instruction through the master's degree, and would admit the top 33 percent of California's high school graduates. Campuses would be largely regional, meaning they would serve surrounding communities rather than far-away cities, or other states or nations. The UC system, in contrast, would become the state's primary agency for research, and offer graduate instruction through the doctorate degree to the top 12.5 percent of high school graduates. Finally, the CCC system would offer lower division academic and vocational courses, potentially culminating in two-year academic degrees that prepared students for the UC or CSU system. The CCC system would provide an "open door" to all high school graduates, including older persons returning to school.

Until 1997 there was no such thing as "strategic planning" at the CSU level. Most planning was traditional in the sense that it was based on budget extrapolations from previous years, rather than strategic choices made to better position the CSU for the future. Strategic planning did, however, exist at the campus level and was typically initiated by university presidents. Such activities, however, were not required or monitored by the chancellor's office.

The Interview Sample

Between November 2002 and January 2003, we interviewed presidents from 11 CSU campuses that ranged considerably in terms of size, age, and so on (see Table 4.1). The largest campus included in the sample was CSU Northridge, with a headcount of over 33,000 students in 2002, while the smallest was CSU San Marcos, with 7,678 students. We also interviewed the current CSU chancellor, Charles Reed, as well as two vice chancellors in order to obtain an administrative perspective of the issues studied. Finally, we interviewed the past CSU chancellor, Barry Munitz (who presided as chancellor from 1991 to 1997 before leaving to become president and CEO of the J. Paul Getty Trust), as well as Thomas Ehrlich (a former university president who played a key role in the CSU strategic planning effort). To obtain a historical perspective (see Table 4.1).

External Environmental Forces

Interviews with the 11 campus presidents revealed a variety of environmental forces that presidents viewed as having a significant impact on the CSU's future. Table 4.2 lists the forces, identified in the order of their priority.

Table 4.1

California State University Campuses Included in the Study

Name	Title	Organization	Size (2002 full-time equivalent enrollment)	Commuter or Residential	Formal Strategic Planning Process Under Way at Campus, at Time of Interview
Jolene Koester	President	Northridge	24,816	Commuter	no
Milton Gordon	President	Fullerton	23,351	Commuter	yes
Bob Caret	President	San Jose	22,186	Commuter	yes
Bob Corrigan	President	San Francisco	21,244	Commuter	yes
John Welty	President	Fresno	17,255	Commuter	yes
Warren Baker	President	San Luis Obispo	17,245	Residential	yes
Bob Suzuki	President	Pomona	16,309	Commuter	yes
Jim Rosser	President	Los Angeles	15,166	Commuter	yes
Manuel Esteban	President	Chico	14,409	Residential	yes
Ruben Arminana	President	Sonoma	7,102	Residential	no
Alex Gonzalez	President	San Marcos	5,826	Commuter	yes
Charles Reed	Chancellor (1998–current)	CSU	—	—	—
Barry Munitz	Chancellor (1991 to 1997)	CSU	—	—	—
David Spence	Executive Vice Chancellor and Chief Academic Officer	CSU	—	—	—
Richard West	Executive Vice Chancellor and Chief Financial Officer	CSU	—	—	—
Thomas Ehrlich	Consultant to Cornerstones; formerly President, Indiana University, and Provost, University of Pennsylvania	Carnegie Foundation	—	—	—

Table 4.2

Environmental Forces

- Demographics
- Economy and Budget
- Technology
- Competition
- Accountability
- Housing Costs

Demographics

The most frequently mentioned force that affects the CSU is changing student demographics. There are two aspects to the demographic change: (1) the unprecedented growth in the numbers of students applying to the CSU system overall, (2) the change in students' ethnic makeup.

Growing Enrollments

Accepting the top one-third of California's high school graduates was feasible until about 2000, when the "Tidal Wave II" (the influx of children of the baby boomer generation) hit. Between 1997 and 2002, enrollment in the CSU rose by 18 percent, to 380,000. By the end of the decade, enrollment is predicted to rise another 26 percent, to 480,000.[1] The strain this is placing on the CSU system is enormous. Charles Reed, the current CSU chancellor, explained: "There are many more students who want to come to the CSU than we have capacity or space for at some of our institutions."

The unprecedented demand threatens to undermine the mission of the CSU, which has been to accept all eligible high school graduates. The chancellor explained: "California policy provides that, if you're in the top third of your high school graduating class you can come to a CSU. There's an expectation. There's a 'right' that people have." Currently the CSU is attempting to respond by operating year-round, offering more classes, and enlarging class size. Ultimately, however, the infrastructure limits will be reached, and measures will have to be taken to cap the number of students CSU campuses can accept. Should this happen, several presidents predicted, it would represent a political nightmare. Jolene Koester, president of CSU Northridge, explained how limiting enrollment will lead to the disenfranchisement of various groups:

> Anything we do to try to control enrollment is going to be seen as disenfranchising various groups. We are the Cal State system—a safety valve for the

social experiment of universal access to higher education that's going on in California and, particularly, in Southern California. Sixty percent of our students are on financial aid. They are predominantly from economically disadvantaged families in this area. If they are denied access to higher education, their parents and their communities are not going to accept the disparity. It is hope that keeps people going, and hope that's based on some real tangible evidence that they can be successful. So, if you close this down and put a cap on enrollments, we're going to have problems.

Changing Ethnic Mix

Not only are enrollments growing, but they are changing drastically in terms of ethnic makeup. The most growth has occurred in the Latino population, which has profound implications for the future of California politics. Chancellor Charles Reed said, "The Latinos are starting to get more political power in the Assembly and in the Senate and in local government." One direct implication of the growing diversity of the student body is pressure on the CSU system to reflect the changes in the faculty. This change has not yet occurred, and may bode problems, especially in the future as the Hispanic population continues to grow. Jim Rosser, the president of CSU Los Angeles, explained:

> The challenge for the University is to try to mirror the demographics of the region we serve. Less than 20 percent of our students are Anglo. It is estimated that Los Angeles County by the year 2015 will be about 30 percent Anglo. If we become a predominantly Hispanic-serving institution in the next 10 years, we may encounter significant difficulty in sustaining a diverse, high quality faculty without a realistic strategic plan, inclusive of an effective enrollment management strategy.

Economy and Budget

The economy was the second most frequently mentioned force by university presidents. About 70 percent of CSU funding comes from the state budget, which is directly tied to the economy. In the early 1990s, times were good. Richard West, the CSU's executive vice chancellor and chief financial officer, said: "In the early '90s the economy was so strong, particularly with the tech sector, that we didn't have to worry—we were given money that was significant—8, 9, 10 percent revenue growth for five or six years."[2] In 2002–2003, rather than the 9.4 percent increase requested by the chancellor, the CSU received a 4.5 percent increase in the general fund. The effect on the CSU system is dramatic. West said "When the economy goes down and the state revenue goes down, our revenue goes down. And we're in a crisis."

Budget crises create different types of problems for the CSU. For instance, it makes it difficult for the CSU to ensure that students graduate on time. Ruben Arminana, the president of CSU Sonoma explained:

> You never know how many resources you can dedicate to the mission of the university. It's a one-semester, two-semester concern. I mean, here we are today not knowing if we're going to get a mid-year reduction. What you do is you manage the best you can, but those uncertainties are a source of tension and continuous concern, and mostly because of uncertainty. If you tell me what it's going to be, I can adjust and deal with that. But not knowing if it's going to be X, or X-1 or X-20, I think is very difficult to do.

Budget crises force the CSU to make cuts somewhere—for instance, in technology or academic services. Chancellor Charles Reed said:

> You know, we're either at the top of the mountain or deep in the valley . . . we're going to hit some bumps in the road and say, OK, maybe we can't implement the technology part. Maybe we can't build these many partnerships with the schools. Maybe we can't provide the kinds of academic services to students that we thought we were going to be able to.

Budget shortfalls place greater pressure on CSU campuses to raise their own money through fund-raising. The chancellor has suggested that campuses need now to put a priority on philanthropy, or fund-raising—up to 10 percent of the general fund. Raising large sums of money can be difficult, however. Manuel Esteban, the president of CSU Chico, said: "I can tell you that raising ten and a half million dollars a year in a place like Chico is a monumental task. . . . In the last two years we've raised five to six million dollars, which is only 5 percent to 6 percent."

Part of the problem is that fund-raising requires a cultural shift for the university. President Esteban explained:

> In order to raise money you have to raise friends. In order to raise friends you have to do a lot of entertaining, a lot of cultivation, and it doesn't get done generally from 8 to 5. And it doesn't get done from Monday to Friday. It gets done in the evening and it gets done on the weekends. And people feel that, you know, they already put in their time at work and the rest of the time should be their own. So it's very, very tough. I don't think that we are professional enough in that area. It's something that we have had to learn to do, and not everybody is good at it. And although we're investing more money, we're not really seeing the results.

Moreover, fund-raising is typically targeted at alumni—a strategy that is problematic at the CSU because, according to one president, CSU alumni are generally not very wealthy. CSU Los Angeles President Rosser explained:

> If we take into consideration that we are a comprehensive university and not a polytechnic, it means that the majority of students who have graduated are social workers, nurses, and teachers—not engineers, architects, lawyers, doctors, or dentists. The latter being individuals who are in a much better position to give, having access to wealth from an alumni/advancement perspective. Consequently, we are working more aggressively to try to prepare students for entry into and success in these areas as well as we face the future.

Technology

Technology was the third most frequently mentioned force. Milton Gordon, president of CSU Fullerton, marveled at the advances, saying: "When I was at the University of Chicago I remember the old computer we had then, which was an analog computer. . . . Now you go around, we have Blackberries and laptops that are the size of a small notebook. It's really been an incredible process." Similarly, Bob Caret, president of San Jose State, commented on how technology has transformed education:

> When the University of Padua was formed in Italy, you'd have a few students sitting around a table with faculty, and that was the typical approach. Now we have all kinds of classes and class arrangements, from labs to clinics to studios to one-on-one, 250 people in a room, distance education on the Web, and a wide range of tools to provide us with yet another way to provide education.

Virtually all campuses provide Internet access to students, and today students routinely use e-mail and the World Wide Web to the point that it is no longer considered a novelty. Sonoma State President Arminana said, "It's now a normal part of life." Several presidents proudly described their efforts to bring their universities into the twenty-first century. Bob Suzuki, the president of Cal State Pomona explained:

> This campus was way, way behind in developing its technological infrastructure, which shocked me when I came here. Even though we're a polytechnic, we were probably in the bottom third of all the campuses in terms of our technology. So we took money off the top, even during the recession, to make sure we caught up, and we're certainly among the top one-

third now. That and the technology initiative taken by the system was help-ful because it really helped us catch up.

Similarly, Milton Gordon, president of Cal State Fullerton, proudly de-scribed his campus's progress:

> State Fullerton is the only one that's ever had a fiber infrastructure totally put in by the State of California. I negotiated that about seven or eight years ago, and I told them, "If you pay for the fiber infrastructure we would do all the top-of-the-ground work." We were also the first ones to have a total digital phone switch, we negotiated our own RFP [request for proposal] and had it put in. We've created all of our classrooms as "smart classrooms," all on our own.

Keeping pace with technology change, however, remains as an unrelent-ing challenge. Cal State Northridge President Koester explained:

> [Technology] is like trying to hold a jellyfish because it can quickly slip through your fingers. You just can't put it in a box. It's changing too fast, and the consequences are changing too fast. I purchased a Blackberry six weeks ago or eight weeks ago because it was the best choice. Now, I prob-ably would make a different choice two months later.

At an organizational or institutional level, keeping up with technology changes often requires making difficult trade-offs. CSU Chico President Esteban said, "When you take into account the infrastructure, software and so on, you are investing a tremendous amount of money, which means you're not investing on somewhere else." One priority for many campuses is invest-ing in instructional delivery, or using technology to provide more or better educational services. Considerable progress has occurred. For example, John Welty, president of CSU Fresno, said "Two years ago we had 600 of our students taking courses that used the Web in some way. This fall, over 16,000 of our students have at least one course or more that uses the Web in one way or another, and that's all within essentially an 18-month period." At many campuses, however, there is still a long way to go. Alex Gonzalez, president of CSU San Marcos, explained:

> We haven't really harnessed the technological ability of the people that we have here to look at the curriculum and to look at delivery. Technology has been more administratively focused—providing people at the desk level with that power, without really adapting it to serving our students better and providing faculty with the ability to do things differently and to make their life easier.

CSU administrators have attempted to encourage faculty to adopt technology by providing incentives for its use. CSU Executive Vice Chancellor David Spence said:

> In higher education, you can't tell faculty how to teach their courses and all that. So instead we make the resources available so people who want to do it can do it. To the extent that faculty want to develop this kind of curriculum, we want to be in a position to support it.

Similarly, several presidents described how they are attempting to facilitate this step. For example, CSU Fresno President Welty, explained:

> We created, for example, a support unit on the campus that's available to work with faculty who want to use the Web as part of their instruction. We're in the midst of providing laptops that are refreshed every three years to all of our faculty. We're renovating our classrooms so that they can use laptops and have access to the Internet and anything else they want during the class.

Competition

Another force, according to several campus presidents, is the arrival of for-profit educational institutions such as University of Phoenix and DeVry. These private universities are now taken seriously by CSU leaders because their programs have been noticed and praised by the business world. San Jose State University President Caret, explained how the arrival of the for-profits has led to a true "paradigm shift" for the CSU:

> In the past, when you were comparing the quality of universities, it had to do largely with inputs—SATs scores, and grants, all the traditional things we've measured, and maybe even the football teams. But these for-profits don't have any of those things. I mean, they're taking pretty much anybody that can walk in the door that's qualified, just like many comprehensives. But, they don't have football teams, they don't even have campuses typically. And yet all of a sudden, the business world is saying, "Hey, these guys are pretty good, you know, I'm going to send my kids to the University of Phoenix."

The for-profits are seen in some cases as superior to Cal State's in terms of class scheduling, time-to-degree, real-world experience of faculty, advising, tutoring, and method of delivery. Bob Corrigan, president of San Francisco State University, said:

I think we're going to be learning from the University of Phoenix in terms of customer service; you talk about user-friendly, being concerned about consumers, the services they provide, the timeliness of what they do, the advising, the tutoring, the class scheduling, where they offer their courses, etc. The fact [is] that nontraditional institutions like Phoenix are much more able to move quickly to create totally new delivery modes, or times or places or ways in which curricula are delivered. We, as an institution, we as a system, have to think a lot more about this.

The entrepreneurial, innovative characteristics of the for-profits also stand in stark contrast to the CSU system. Cal State Northridge President Koester, explained:

Academics and higher education in general are very conservative enter-prises—we are not very nimble or very quick. I think that characteristic already has started to have an impact. It's why you have the successes of the Phoenixes, the Nationals, the Golden Gates, the other entrepreneurial-type institutions, where they're willing to be more flexible in terms of how they offer, what they offer, when they offer, and how they apply academic standards.

CSU leaders at the chancellor's office, however, appeared less worried about the for-profits than these presidents, citing continued demand for the residential model. CSU Executive Vice Chancellor West said:

There are enough people who want the old residential model, and the on-line education market will not replace the old one. I thought that we were going to get a little bit more pressure on the alternative, but the students have kind of voted with their feet and the seats of their pants—they show up in class. . . . Peter Drucker said campuses won't look the same in 20 years . . . I think they will. There will be very different ways technology is going to be used a lot more and other things, but I think in terms of the basic missions, I think it's still going to be there. You're always going to need places to congregate and do certain things.

Another reason the CSU executives don't take the threat seriously is that there is plenty of growth to be had for all. West explained:

Everybody talked about competition in higher education. It just hasn't de-veloped. If anything, particularly for California, the demographics are that some of those competitive alternatives, whether it's at Phoenix or at Na-tional or DeVry, they pick up part of the growth. There's so much growth that there's growth for everybody, and there isn't such a satisfactory or economically attractive alternative that students rush to.

Accountability

While demands for increased public accountability are nothing new for public institutions, several presidents suggested that the recession of the 1990s forced the CSU system to take it more seriously than ever before. For example, CSU Chico President Esteban, explained:

> In the early '90s, we were in very difficult financial straits and there was a possibility of layoffs and so on. Little by little, faculty and everybody else accepted the reality that if we didn't change ourselves, it was going to be imposed on us from the outside. So I think that today there's a kind of a recognition that we have to be constantly in the process of . . . improvement or enhancement—there is less resistance to it now.

Others cite new legislative initiatives as evidence of an ever-growing emphasis on accountability. Koester said:

> Every year there's a new legislature that considers some kind of accountability mechanism or a process for state institutions. I think this will remain an ongoing concern. Look at what Pat Callan has done with the National Center for Public Policy and Higher Education, and its use of report cards. Pat Callan and the important issues he is raising aren't going to go away. He represents that trend.[3]

Koester suggested that in the future, universities will need to demonstrate that they use the public's money for the public good, just as health care institutions have been forced to do:

> What's happened in health care and other publicly supported entities is going to happen in higher education. Students and legislators no longer accept our saying, "You need to do this because we say so." They want to know why, and what's the outcome. And I think we're going to have increasing pressures to demonstrate that what we're doing accomplishes our stated goals, and we're going to have to be able to demonstrate that we use the public's money well, and to good end.

One concern in the area of accountability is graduation rates. CSU Executive Vice Chancellor David Spence explained: "I'm troubled by the fact that our average student takes nearly 150 units before they graduate and all they need is 120. I mean, if I were a state legislator, I'd be on that one!"

While they acknowledge the need for greater accountability, some presidents caution that going too far would lead to problems associated with bureaucracies. San Jose State President Caret said:

> We get a huge amount of public support and funding, and we should be held accountable. But I get very, very nervous when intervention of government gets so strong that we could be changed into a state agency, more like K–12. And we've all seen the lack of creativity and drive that can occur when you become a giant bureaucracy, as opposed to a creative institution. For that reason, I do think that accountability and state oversight is something to be worried about.

Some presidents maintain that higher education has already become too much like K–12, in which teachers are forced to engage in numerous accountability-related activities. Caret explained:

> You hear a typical elementary school teacher and high school teacher saying, "These are all the reports I have to prepare and these are the things that are being demanded of me by either the principal or the superintendent or the statewide Board of Education." Now higher education is facing the same thing. We're making demands on faculty for assessment activities, attempts to internationalize the campus, more attention to community service and community service learning, all of which are important from a larger perspective. But the faculty see it as interfering with their control of what goes on in the classroom, and their independence as faculty members.

Housing Costs

According to several presidents, housing costs will make it difficult to replace the large cohort of faculty which was hired in the 1960s and 1970s during the CSU system's early growth. The impact of housing costs is felt especially in urban areas such as the Bay Area or Los Angeles. San Francisco State President Corrigan explained:

> The statistic I cite a lot is that when the faculty who are now retiring in San Francisco took their jobs, the medium-priced home was roughly three times the starting salary of an assistant professor. That is no longer the case, even for people coming in at higher administrative salaries.

Similarly, CSU San Marcos President Gonzalez offered some dire statistics:

Very, very important is the cost of living here, and, you know, like Northridge or L.A., how can you recruit and hire new faculty if they can't afford a house? I mean, the average price in San Diego now has just skyrocketed, and at San Marcos the average price for an existing home is like $384,000. The new ones will start out at $400,000 and above. So how do you get an assistant professor, or even an associate professor, if they don't have two incomes? That's going to be a real, real big problem for us right here.

The Pace of Change: Turbulence? What Turbulence?

As noted in chapter 1, a working hypothesis of this study was that the external environment would be perceived as more turbulent than in years past. By and large we found this not to be the case in the CSU. For example, CSU Pomona President Suzuki said, "I wouldn't characterize the environment as turbulent. I think there's some chaos there, certainly, but I wouldn't call it turbulence. Rather, I would say the environment is changing very rapidly." Many presidents, in fact, instead described their universities' environments as relatively controlled and manageable. CSU Fullerton President Gordon suggested that this difference stems from the public versus private sector. He said:

> I think that the use of the words "turbulence" and "chaos" creates a problem. We don't use them. We have challenges. We have probably as much, or more, of the changes that occur in private corporations, but we handle them with a different attitude, I think, towards them. So we would not begin by saying, "This is a chaotic event. We're getting all these new students. They're younger. What can we do with them?" We just accept the challenge and then see how we can sit down and work through them.

Several presidents suggested that universities seek to maintain unruffled even in situations of budget crisis, rather than be buffeted by environmental change. Gordon said:

> Every day there's going to be new challenges, and you have to decide to try and maintain your mission, your goals, in the face of these challenges. And we have. They're not a disaster to throw us off course or anything like that. When we plan budgets we don't do budget planning one year at a time— we do multiyears. We try and look at the long range, over several years.

At root appears to be the goal of preserving universities as "islands of calm" in an otherwise turbulent world. San Jose State President Caret explained how this is accomplished by the notion of "buffering" the university from outside forces—which he advocated:

Buffering campuses [from external turbulence] is really critical. I mean, one of the beauties of an academic world—and it's probably true in some parts of the business world, particularly in the R&D sector—is, we are islands of calm. In other words, you can take an esoteric topic, and we can sit here and discuss it for two or three years and spend a lot of time and substance simply for the sake of discussing it. And I don't think universities can lose that ability, otherwise they are no longer, in my mind, universities. They need to be places where people can reflect and reflective thought occurs, debate occurs, and the stimulation of new ideas occurs. We are not here just to serve the public in terms of providing a work force, for example, or certification. That's part of what we do today, because we are public universities. But we don't want to lose that traditional role of universities in the process.

CSU Northridge President Koester explained that universities' conservative nature derives from the quest for truth, the value placed on shared government, and the system of faculty tenure:

In higher education, there is a strong value on continuity, and a strong value on keeping things the way they are because there's a belief in the absolute truth of our mission as educators. So there's a lot of resistance to rapid-fire change. I think, as well, that we see in higher education institutions almost an insulation from forces of change because of the value we place on shared governance and how we do our work, which are really important values. Also, because our faculty generally stay at one place for most of their career, if we did something ten years ago and it failed or succeeded, or something in between, there's understandably a feeling we should never try it again. So, universities are not very flexible in response to change.

An outgrowth of the pursuit of stability is the belief that universities should respond to their environments slowly, steadily, and deliberately, rather than be "whipsawed" by rapid and unpredictable environmental change. Any proposed response to environmental change, presidents suggested, must be contemplated deeply, consensually, and at great length before execution. Sonoma State President Arminana explained:

The academics' attitude toward change is that change is gradual, and we ought to take our time and analyze it and study it, thinking of all of the possible ramifications, and put it into a plan, and be sure we have consensus, and so everybody is aboard and happy.

For those trying to bring about change in the university, such as the chancellor's office, higher education's conservative nature can be a source of frustration. Chancellor Reed, for instance, said "We should change faster. But we have a different governance system [than the private sector], a whole different set of expectations about involvement. Our governance system can be cumbersome." Executive Vice Chancellor David Spence agreed with the chancellor about the pace of change not being fast enough. On occasion, he said, he wishes the legislature would just pass a law, forcing the CSU to speed up:

> There are some things I am very frustrated about. Like our relationship with the community colleges, at least with respect to helping students negotiate the process of obtaining the baccalaureate degree. Every once in a while I'm tempted to just go to the legislature and say, "Pass a law. You know, make us do it." You know, we resisted doing that, because it's not really the way we like to do things.

Sonoma State President Arminana suggested that despite the accelerated pace of change, universities have changed little for the past 800 years:

> The pace of change has accelerated. It is the only constant. I read that the rate of information and knowledge doubles about every 70 days. Well I have cheese in my refrigerator that is older than 70 days! There's no more conservative institution than the academy. The academy has been here now for 800 years and we have survived . . . we are second only to the Church, who was our Mother. And our record of surviving and contributing has been pretty good. So people say, I have done it this way successfully, for the last 20 years. Why should we change now?

History and Evolution of the Strategy Process

Impetus for Strategy Process

Before 1997 there was no such thing as systemwide strategic planning at the CSU. Strategic planning was conducted at the level of individual campuses, typically at the discretion of individual campus presidents. The first-ever campuswide strategic planning effort began in 1997 when then-chancellor Barry Munitz's vision for the future coincided with a unique opportunity to conduct strategic planning campus-wide. Munitz had long viewed strategic planning as a way to bring about better alignment between individual campuses, the CSU system, and the external environment:

> Given the size and complexity of the Cal State system, we had always been talking about the balance between campus priorities and system overall objectives. One of the questions was, how does the system level support and encour-

age and facilitate campus-level planning? At the same time, particularly as resources were getting tighter, how do we approach some of the essentials or nuclear questions from a system basis? In our case, it was really trying to match the highest priorities for the institution internally with the changing external factors related to money and politics, and the interest of the state. Externally, you had a changing legislature, term limits, demographics, and an economic crisis. Internally, it was research versus economic development versus undergraduate education versus teacher training . . . so we had to bring in to much closer alignment the external and the internal priorities.

Unlike the other two organizations in this study, the CSU faced no "burning platform." Rather, the impetus was growth and continuous improvement.[4] Former CSU chancellor Munitz explained:

Life would have gone on had we not embarked on strategic planning; it wasn't a survival issue. It was an improvement and enhancement issue. Unlike corporations like H-P, which live and die by quarterly P&L [profit and loss] statements, and the County, which is strapped with public money, the CSU was going to go on. The classrooms, laboratories, athletic fields, and concert halls would all continue to exist, but the question is, Would they be focused? Would they be strengthened? Would they grow? And would we be able to match resources to greatest need?

Munitz's desire to engage in strategic planning coincided with a joint invitation from the Association of Governing Boards and the Pew Trusts Higher Education Round Table. These two organizations had just completed a national roundtable discussion about the external forces facing universities and the need to reframe higher education for the future. They asked the CSU to participate in the project, and to be the first example of a highly participatory, public, multicampus strategic planning effort that involved trustees and faculty in deliberations about future plans and decisions. Munitz explained:

We were approached by the PEW Trust, who said they were interested in the same question as we were. They wanted at least one participant in a strategic planning effort they were funding that was a multicampus system, to see whether it was even possible. And so, that was how we then specifically got into Cornerstones [the campus-wide strategic planning effort].

Formation of Cornerstones

Munitz began by pulling together a planning group of 24 members that included CSU trustees, faculty, students, presidents, and senior CSU system administrators. The group was chaired by Thomas Ehrlich, formerly provost of the University of Pennsylvania and president of Indiana University, which had also engaged in a university-wide strategic planning effort. Just getting the 24-member group to work together was a challenge. Munitz recalled:

> The key was getting so many different constituencies around the table, and having them understand each other's context, history, and biases. To have faculty and students suddenly engaging board members, to have the administration feel that their authority wasn't being undermined by this separate but very special effort, and to have about 25 people who normally never had a chance to spend good quality personal time together avoid getting off track because they were establishing separate agendas—was quite a challenge.

The planning group's first task was to identify four underlying principles, or "cornerstones," that would form the foundation for the CSU's commitment to the State of California. These were as follows:

- Provide the highest standards of undergraduate education.
- Meet the demand for higher education in California with the available resources.
- Answer to the people of California and be accountable for its performance.
- Serve the changing educational needs of the state and its people.

Four task forces were then formed to flesh out each of the four principles and to develop a draft of the Cornerstones Report. Each task force included members of the planning group and partners from the broader CSU community and beyond. Emphasis was placed on making the process open and transparent in order to build trust among the various constituents. Thomas Ehrlich, who chaired the Cornerstones planning group, explained:

> Munitz charged us over the next 18 months to two years with coming up with an academic plan that would strengthen teaching and learning, research and service on all the campuses. We wanted to find ways to give everyone who we could, a chance to express thoughts, concerns, issues— students, faculty, staff—and to build a sense of collaborative undertaking. The process, what we were doing, was very open and transparent. There were no efforts to do other than say to everybody, "Here's where it is, here's the next version," and have an interactive process. We spent a lot of time on that. This enabled us to gain a sense of ownership from faculty, from trustees, students, in the process and in the outcomes, in a way that enabled us to actually end up with a set of proposals and standards for

undergraduate education, graduate education, research and service that everyone thought would strengthen and help the CSU.

Over the course of a year, findings from the task force were discussed at the academic senate and at campus-based forums and meetings. Feedback was gathered and incorporated into the final draft of the report, which was unanimously approved by the California Board of Trustees and endorsed as the systemwide planning framework on January 28, 1998.

The Cornerstones Report

The Cornerstones Report contained four policy goals (which grew out of the four Cornerstones), ten guiding principles, and specific recommendations intended to help campuses shape their futures. (The policy goals and 10 guiding principles are shown in Table 4.3; see the Cornerstones Report for specific recommendations.)

The report clearly acknowledged campus's existing strategic planning efforts and explained that Cornerstones would simply tie together such efforts and provide an overarching framework that would enhance public understanding of the CSU's mission and needs. This intent is clearly spelled out in the following section of the Cornerstones Report (p. 3):

> Cornerstones has been designed to complement and support campus strategic planning initiatives that are ongoing on the CSU campuses. It is an umbrella effort that has been informed by and in many cases has grown out of campus-level initiatives that are already in place. But what has been missing, and what Cornerstones seeks to supply, is an overarching set of statewide goals and plans that will be a framework for both articulating the needs and accounting for the contributions of the university to a larger statewide public and policy audience.

Rather than mandate a certain approach to strategic planning, Cornerstones explicitly stipulated that "the California State University campuses shall have significant autonomy in developing their own missions, identity, and programs, with institutional flexibility in meeting clearly defined system policy goals" (p. 16, Principle 10). Former chancellor Munitz explained:

> There is no right answer [regarding how to do strategic planning]. It depends on context, an individual's style, and on the history, size, and complexity of the institution. It would be dangerous to assume that one size fits all. You have to take on the one hand your list of conditions and require-

Table 4.3

Cornerstones Goals and Principles

A. Ensuring Educational Results

1. The California State University will award the baccalaureate on the basis of demonstrated learning as determined by our faculty. The CSU will state explicitly what a graduate of the CSU is expected to know, and will assure that our graduates possess a certain breadth and depth of knowledge together with a certain level of skills, and are exposed to experiences that encourage the development of sound personal values.
2. Students are the focus of the academic enterprise. Each campus will shape the provision of its academic programs and support services to better meet the diverse needs of its students and society.
3. Students will be expected to be active partners with faculty in the learning process, and the university will provide opportunities for active learning throughout the curriculum.
4. The CSU will reinvest in its faculty to maintain its primary mission as a teaching-centered comprehensive university. Faculty scholarship, research and creative activity are essential components of that mission.

B. Ensuring Access to Higher Education

5. The CSU will meet the need for undergraduate education in California through increasing outreach efforts and transfer, retention, and graduation rates, and providing students a variety of pathways that may reduce the time needed to complete degrees.
6. Graduate education and continuing education are essential components of the mission of the California State University.

C. Ensuring Financial Stability

7. The State of California must develop a new policy framework for higher education finance to assure that the goals of the Master Plan are met. This framework should be the basis for the subsequent development of periodic "compacts" between the State and the institutions of higher education.
8. The responsibility for enhancing educational excellence, access, diversity, and financial stability shall be shared by the State, the California State University system, the campuses, our faculty and staff, and students.

D. Ensuring University Accountability

9. The California State University will account for its performance in facilitating the development of its students, in serving the communities in which we reside, and in the continued contribution to the California economy and society, through regular assessment of student achievement, and through periodic reports to the public regarding our broader performance.
10. The California State University campuses shall have significant autonomy in developing their own missions, identity, and programs, with institutional flexibility in meeting clearly defined system policy goals.

Source: Cornerstones Report, www.calstate.edu/AcadAff/accountability/index.shtml, p. 19.

ments, and on the other hand the possible ways to proceed, and then be thoughtful and be honest about making the match.

Campuses were, however, to be held accountable for meeting Cornerstones' goals. Executive Vice Chancellor Spence explained:

> We don't have a requirement that [campuses] do strategic planning. But they won't say "no" to us if it's Cornerstones, because that's what the Board [of Trustees] adopted. We have these very clear recommendations, we have schedules, who does what, what is a campus's responsibility for this, what's the system responsibility, and a whole accountability process. So they wouldn't say no.

Reflections on the Process of Developing Cornerstones

The most difficult part of developing Cornerstones, according to those involved, was the process—particularly enacting the collegial, participatory model of shared governance on which university cultures are based. Former chancellor Munitz said:

> The hardest part was getting started and establishing the ground rules. The next most difficult part was the planning process itself. The easiest part— and I might add, in my own cynical judgment, the least essential part—was the product.

One difficulty, for example, was faculty members' expectation that they, rather than administrators, determine campus priorities. CSU Northridge President Koester explained:

> I saw Cornerstones as an attempt to try to do planning at the system level, bringing together the trustees, the faculty and the administration. This is a very, very difficult objective to accomplish, because the strong sense in the CSU is that the faculty need to be the stimulus, rather than the reactor; that the faculty need to determine [objectives], and then other constituencies need to respond. I recollect tensions around that difference in perception about the appropriate role of the various constituent groups in a strategic planning process, tensions that reared their head fairly repeatedly throughout the course of the discussions.

Over time, however, according to Thomas Ehrlich, Munitz was able to convince faculty members and others that the process could be win-win, and therefore he deserves much of the credit for the completion of Cornerstones. Ehrlich explained:

Munitz was able to persuade the faculty senate of the university that this was a good idea, and nothing would be done if the faculty didn't think it was a good idea. . . . Barry Munitz certainly was the one who persuaded these groups that this could really happen and it could be good for everybody and certainly good for the university. It was a really remarkable process that couldn't have happened without Barry Munitz. He was able to bring together faculty members and trustees—trustees were invited to come talk to the faculty. That had never happened before. There were lots of discussions and debates, with a real sense of collaboration and common mission that was enhanced as a result of the journey.

Ehrlich agreed with Munitz: "The journey was at least as important as the outcomes, and in lots of ways probably more important."

Implementation of Cornerstones

In 1998 Charles Reed replaced Barry Munitz as chancellor of the CSU system, and inherited the task of implementing Cornerstones. At the time, said Executive Vice Chancellor Spence, Cornerstones was so comprehensive and high level that the next steps were not clear. Spence recalled: "It was pretty obvious that there wasn't any idea of how to implement it, or commitment to do so [on the part of campuses], for that matter. . . . So first thing that we had to do was to develop some kind of implementation plan, and in doing so, kind of energize the system."

The first step was to prioritize the myriad goals and recommendations contained in the Cornerstones Report. Spence explained: One of our problems with the original Cornerstones was that there was too much in it. . . . So we needed to give greater weight to certain things and lesser weight to the others." The second step was to translate the high-level goals into concrete action items. Both steps were accomplished through the development of the "Implementation Plan," which took more than a year to produce. According to Chancellor Reed, the process was long and arduous, but well worth it at the end. The chancellor explained: "It took us 18 months to get an Implementation Plan, which was frustrating to me—but in the academic arena, you know, going slow and following the process is important." The result was a document that tied the Cornerstones recommendations to timelines and completion dates.[5] According to Chancellor Reed, "We honored the academic process, and at the end of 18 months, we had this roadmap with milestones on it that clearly outlined where we needed to go so that we could report every other year to the board and demonstrate our accountability."

Table 4.4

California State University Institutional Performance Areas

1. Quality of baccalaureate degree programs
2. Access to the CSU
3. Progression to the degree
4. Graduation
5. Areas of special state need
6. Relations with K-12
7. Remediation
8. Facilities utilization
9. University advancement
10. Quality of graduate and postbaccalaureate programs
11. Faculty scholarship and creative achievement
12. Contributions to community and society
13. Institutional effectiveness

Source: www.calstate.edu/Cornerstones/reports/ProAcctProcess.html.

The Accountability Process

The last step was to develop a process to ensure that campuses remained accountable to the goals contained in Cornerstones. This was accomplished through the development of a final document called the "Accountability Process," which specified that (1) each individual campus would be accountable to the Board of Trustees and chancellor; and (2) the CSU system would be held accountable to the general public and its governing bodies—specifically, 13 institutional performance areas based on the mission of the CSU and its campuses (see Table 4.4). Campuses were required to demonstrate accountability by turning in reports on a regular basis, documenting their activities. These reports are available on the California State University official Web site.[6]

Reflections on the Process of Implementing Cornerstones

While Cornerstones is now more than five years old, CSU executives believe it is still very much alive. Executive Vice Chancellor Spence said "We've kept on course. We've kept Cornerstones in front of people, and we refer back to it all the time." Similarly, Chancellor Reed believes the strategic plan is "still as vital, important and strategic today, as it was five years ago." Moreover, he uses it regularly to keep the system aligned:

> There are 13 major goals in this strategic plan. Over the last five years, I have continued to use Cornerstones and those major goals to help

drive the decisions, the policies, the budget in the California State University system.

Chancellor Reed considers the plan his "bible" and relies on it to create a sense of order and consistency:

> The strategic plan is really important because with boards, with presidents, with subsidiaries, you can always return to the plan if it's a good plan, and stick with the plan. As I said to the Board yesterday, "The plan is my constitution, my charter, and I stick with that." And that's why it's not bad to come back and read it every once in a while, or, to use it again and again.

While most campuses readily accepted the plan on paper, making sure they actively align themselves with it remains the most important part. Chancellor Reed explained:

> I think that most of the universities, although they may be on a different schedule, have bought into Cornerstones. They bought into the accountability reporting and the schedule because we really built the schedule with them, and they take an ownership of that. Now it's important for the universities to communicate the accountability measures throughout their organizations.

Chancellor Reed aims to drive the plan downward both through personal conviction and through the university's administrative structure:

> It gets communicated by, one, me being an advocate, and speaking out in favor of it. But it also gets communicated through the vice chancellors in their functional areas. We have an Academic Affairs organization. And we have an executive vice chancellor who heads that. Then he brings the provosts together. He brings the deans together. And so we try to make sure it gets communicated.

When asked what is the hardest part of driving the plan downward, Chancellor Reed explained that faculty members have no real incentive to engage in strategic planning, especially given their already busy lives:

> Faculty members are loyal to their discipline [rather than to their institutions]. Their reward system comes through their disciplines. We have 22,000 faculty members, and they work hard to do their research, and their publishing, and their teaching. And then when you come in and say, "We want you to do [strategic planning] . . . ," it's an add-on to their lives.

Strategy at the Campus Level

We now turn to campus presidents to find out how Cornerstones, and strategic planning more generally, is viewed at their level. What are presidents' views of Cornerstones, and what impact has it had on their campuses?

Awareness of Cornerstones

More than five years after it was unveiled, while Cornerstones is no longer discussed as a topic of conversation *per se*, most presidents agreed that its implementation continues. Sonoma State President Arminana said "Even though I don't think the word Cornerstones is as often in the mouths of people as it was a number of years ago, its implementation remains very much alive." Similarly, CSU San Marcos President Gonzalez said "You know, I don't hear very much at all. I hear a little from select campuses. And it's not really a topic of conversation with the president. But I know people are engaged in it." According to San Francisco State President Bob Corrigan, Cornerstones remains a viable planning guide:

> We don't sit there and talk about Cornerstones unto itself, but if there's a topic that comes up that relates to something in Cornerstones, Cornerstones is clearly invoked in the dialogue around that particular issue—for example, especially the yearly assessment. It does remain a very viable part of our planning and gives the broad guidelines as to where we're moving.

One situation in which Cornerstones is often discussed is during campuses' reaccreditation processes, which require campuses to engage in strategic planning. CSU Los Angeles President Rosser explained:

> Cornerstones might come up within the context of accreditation, because the Western Association of Colleges and Schools (WASC) now expects evidence of a strategic planning process that is participatory and that institutional progress toward achieving strategic goals and objectives is occurring.

Interestingly, one president suggested that Cornerstones becomes less viable over time as the environment changes. CSU Nortridge President Koester said:

> [Cornerstones] was certainly referred to far more often three years ago than it is now. So the frequency has decreased as we are further out from the plan itself. And I think that's appropriate. You know, the shelf life of

something like this is not going to be much longer than where we are right now. The circumstances have changed too much.

Impact of Cornerstones

During discussions with presidents, we asked, What has been the impact of Cornerstones on your campuses. Clearly its biggest impact has been establishing a sense of accountability. For instance, Cal Poly Pomona President Suzuki said, "One of the things that Cornerstones did was emphasize outcomes assessment, which helped us because we had been trying to push that ourselves." Similarly, Bob Caret, San Jose State's president said, "The entire leadership team is very familiar with and understands what Cornerstones was trying to achieve. We are assessed every year on many of the Cornerstones criteria; it stays in front of us all the time."

Increasingly, accountability is built into campuses' curricular activities. For instance, CSU San Marcos President Gonzalez said:

> I think the greatest impact Cornerstones had for us is that it's instituting a level of accountability that wasn't there before. What I'd like to do is to take it one step further, so that as we develop new programs, and as we look at the curriculum, and as we do the other things, that we ensure that we have measurements, analysis, and accountability in there. That's what hasn't been there in the past.

The focus on accountability also translates into planning and budget activities. CSU Los Angeles President Rosser explained:

> Every CSU campus now has indicators of success that it is expected to achieve. Cornerstones provides a backdrop against which planning occurs within the university. In many instances, campus strategic initiatives are tied to progressive goals that have been established with regard to Cornerstones. For example, if we say we are going to increase the number of first-time freshmen who don't need remediation, there may be some reallocation or some additional resources that we may need to commit to achieve this initiative— whether it means materials we use to market and advertise the university, adding new outreach staff, or setting targets with respect to the number of students we hope would enter with scores above 1,400 on the SAT or who have graduated in the top 1 percent of their high school graduating class.

Cornerstones had a direct impact at CSU Los Angeles by prompting the campus to establish an assessment unit within one of its programs. President Rosser explained:

We have had to establish a learning outcomes assessment unit within our Center for Effective Teaching and Learning (CETL), because Cornerstones asserts that the CSU will grant the Baccalaureate on the basis of demonstrated learning. We are establishing student learning outcomes expectations for every program and every course. In order to accomplish the preceding, resources had to be found to establish a unit that would provide support and assistance, and at the same time monitor progress toward the achievement of our goals.

Awareness of other Cornerstones themes remains heightened as well. For example, Sonoma State President Arminana said "Items of Cornerstones remain very active and in play—for example concern for access, retention, and teacher education." Similarly, San Jose State President Caret said

I wouldn't say we keep Cornerstones under our pillows and pull it out every time something is going on, but I'm pretty tenacious about not letting plans just die after they're written. So I bring Cornerstones out on a regular basis in terms of some of the key issues, whether it be how we handle graduate fees in the future, or the role of graduate programs in the CSU, some of the fiscal issues we talked about, why all of those kinds of things are playing a role clearly in what we do also.

Campus-Level Strategic Planning Activities

As noted earlier, while Cornerstones required campuses to engage in accountability activities, it did not require that campuses engage in strategic planning activities. Many campuses had, however, already done so prior to Cornerstones. In such cases, merging campuses' planning activities with Cornerstones was effortless. For example, Chico State President Esteban explained:

We preceded Cornerstones, and to our great satisfaction a lot of the work that Cornerstones wanted to accomplish was something that we had already done. So when we were asked to put together a plan on how we would implement Cornerstones, we basically sent our strategic plan. So for us, it was, fortuitously, something that was very easy for us to do. . . . Cornerstones was something that we actually adopted after our strategic plan, rather than vice versa.

At another campus, strategic planning activities coincided with Cornerstones perfectly. San Francisco State President Corrigan said:

We are in Phase 2 of the strategic planning effort that started some years ago. . . . From the get-go we were very much aware of what was going on with Cornerstones. As we were moving ahead with our strategic planning, we literally we had a draft of Cornerstones [in front of us]. If you look at our published strategic plan, you'll see down the left-hand columns quotations that we actually pulled out of Cornerstones, so our recommendations line up directly with Cornerstones' themes.

Not all campuses, however, have chosen to engage in formal strategic planning, for various reasons. CSU Chico President Esteban explained:

> I'm not sure that every campus has done strategic planning. I think that every campus has to do more or less what the Cornerstones requires and what the accountability reports require. But I think that you would find great, great diversions from campus to campus. . . . So I think you would find that, although some campuses may have done strategic planning, they don't necessarily follow that strategic plan. And most of them don't even have a strategic plan.

At CSU Northridge, for example, President Koester decided against continuing the existing strategic planning effort when she arrived, largely because of its negative reputation:

> Frankly, the reaction to strategic planning that I received from so many people during the six months that I was a president-in-waiting, was so strong and was so negatively balanced, that I gave that up. When I said the words "strategic plan," people moved away from me in conversation in a nonverbal manner. And I thought, you know, this is not a good legacy to build on.

Sonoma State President Arminana shuns strategic planning for a different reason—because, he believes, the process can't keep up with a rapidly changing environment:

> I'm not the greatest fan of strategic planning. I am not a great believer in these complex, detailed, lots-of-people, lots-of-paper, very nicely put together plans that, by the time you have finished them the world has changed. Often, they are placed on a very nice bookshelf they gather dust until either you have the next plan and you take the old one and move it out and put the new one in. Look, anybody who did strategic planning based on the state of California funding a year ago is back in rewrite, because the funding picture changed literally in a period of 120 days. During convocation in the fall, we were talking about large amounts of surpluses. By convocation in January I was saying, "guys, all the signals are going the other way! It won't happen!"

Most presidents supported campus autonomy regarding strategic planning activities. Several, however, also believed that at least some type of strategic planning should be mandated at every campus, and that such efforts be documented so that the system level can keep better track of campus activities. CSU Los Angeles President Rosser said:

> Having argued for campus flexibility in the establishment of indicators of success, each campus is to file its strategic plan and to provide yearly progress reports to the campus and to the chancellor's office.

Themes and Issues at the Campus Level

From discussions with presidents about the strategic processes under way at their campuses, several cross-cutting themes emerged. These are discussed below.

The Participative Approach

As noted earlier, Cornerstones did not mandate any particular approach to strategic planning. Regardless, virtually all campuses that *were* engaged in strategic planning (9 out of 11) employed a highly collegial, participative approach that entailed obtaining broad participation from campus constituents in order to gain buy-in into the strategic planning process. This was usually accomplished through the establishment of some type of Strategic Planning Committee or Commission, which typically included the provost, vice presidents of various academic units, members of the Academic Senate, deans of colleges, as well as representatives from the faculty and staff. Efforts also often included representatives from the student body as well as the community through the establishment of business councils or task forces. According to many presidents, the importance of such broad-based participation cannot be overstated. San Francisco President Corrigan explained that many campuses' strategic planning efforts go awry because the process is too "top heavy," or dominated by administrators and consultants with little faculty or staff input. As a result, there is little buy-in from those who are expected to actually implement the plan. To avoid the pitfalls of a top-heavy approach, Corrigan consciously made the process as participative, or "grass roots" as possible. He explained:

> We believed that essential to a strategic plan that wouldn't gather dust, that faculty would buy into, and that would have some impact on the institution, was grassroots involvement. That's why something like 300 faculty

members—that's almost 50 percent of the full-time faculty—were involved in those various task forces. For example, the academic excellence task force met for like a year and a half, every Friday afternoon, for two hours. There were never fewer than 30 faculty members at one of those sessions. So that aspect of it came off very well.

Obtaining broad-based participation can take a long time, and lengthen the time required to make decisions. However, as San Jose State President Caret pointed out, the time investment is worth it because it results in a healthier decision:

People get frustrated with academe because we go through these sorts of shared governance dialogues that make it look like nobody can make a decision. But really what we're doing is making a healthier decision. We can make fast decisions if we have to, but if we don't have to, we don't feel the pressure of making fast decisions. We feel like it's more important to take the time to discuss, and in the long run we wind up with a stronger and healthier campus.

Similarly, CSU Fresno President Welty said: "The broad-based involvement, using ten task forces, opening it up to anybody who wants to join was a cumbersome process that takes time—but in our institutional culture, it's very important." Based on his experience, CSU Chico President Esteban believes that the strategic planning process has to be democratic in order to succeed:

Even though I was the one who initiated the process, it is a process that has to appear to be something that stems from the grass roots. This is why the committee had representatives from every group and had a majority of faculty, so that at the end it was the recommendation from the faculty, the staff, the students, and the community that became the strategic plan of the university. . . . A strategic plan has to be something that is endorsed by those people who are going to have to live the consequences of it. So you have to have a fairly comprehensive approach to it, and it has to be collaborative and it has to be accepted. People have to buy into it.

The Charette Process

One specific participative technique used by a number of presidents is the "charette" process, the purpose of which is to facilitate large-group decision-making. In a charette, constituents are first broken into groups, each of which addresses a key topic area. Following a step-by-step process, each group reviews and refines the progress made by each of the other groups so that all groups become familiar with all issues. Eventually the results of each topic area discussion are folded into a draft document or proposal, which is later given back to the constituents. According to Warren Baker, San Luis Obispo president, charettes help avoid the tendency for group meetings to turn into "public hearings where angry constituents voice concerns in an adversarial manner that increases the likelihood that they will be overlooked or dismissed." Baker explained and provided an example:

> As we focus on a specific element of the plan, we'll have a charette. For example, we convened a charette in planning for expansion of the northwest section of the campus. This proposed expansion has implications for Foundation services, recreation, technology, the library, and for engineering laboratory facilities. A charette is organized to include all of the players, so that each hears all the issues. It's a very open event, generally facilitated by an outside professional. In some cases we have even brought donors in, people who are underwriting the total cost of the building, so that our conversation with the donor about that building is not isolated but part of an overall planning process.

Baker explained how the charette process ensures that a "meeting of the minds" occurs in terms of what's being done and why:

> Of course tensions arise, but we've been able to solve them with this concept of a charette. For instance, when everyone has the opportunity to completely review the plans for academic expansion, everyone comes to recognize that there are more than just new classroom and laboratory facilities involved. There are more than just residence halls. There is quality of life for students on the campus, there's the support infrastructure, there's a laundry, there's a movie theater, all of these things are issues that need to be taken into account. And so various parts of the university, like the Foundation, business affairs, recreational sports, and so on, come prominently into play. The charette helps us a great deal to achieve a meeting of the minds regarding both where we're going and "why" things are done.

At CSU Fresno, the charette process was also key. President Welty explained how it was used to come up with a first draft of the university strategic plan:

> Ten task forces were organized around major topical areas, such as faculty, academic programs, engagement with the community students, et cetera. Their responsibility is to generate a set of recommendations in the area

they're working in. Then those recommendations come forward in a day-long process in which we use a charette process to review all the recommendations to the task forces. And out of that charette comes the modified document that eventually is a first draft of the university plan. And then the monitoring or steering committee does a review of that first draft and modifications are made and it goes back out to the task force chairs. They make comments, and then finally the steering committee moves forward a plan that goes to the Academic Senate for their endorsement, and once that's endorsed we ask the vice president and deans, the heads of the major areas to assume responsibility for implementing specific parts of that plan. And the steering committee oversees, and requires an annual report, oversees the monitoring.

Welty identified the charette process as a best practice that he would advocate to others:

The charette process has served us very well. That's the day we announced that for the entire day we were going to address the recommendations coming from the task forces. Anybody can come, and they all have feedback forms they can make comments on, so it does help to let everyone know they can be involved if they choose to be involved and that if they do choose to be involved, at least whatever they have to say or they write down will be considered. It's definitely a best practice that I'd recommend to others.

Ongoing, Multiphase, Multiyear

Another characteristic common to many campuses' strategic planning process was the tendency for them to be ongoing and multiphase in nature, sometimes spanning up to 10 years as well as multiple presidents' tenures. CSU Fresno President Welty has led the strategic planning process three times at his campus over the last 11 years. The process, he explained, has become a "major part of our university's activity." Welty explained its cyclical nature:

Every three to five years we engage the university community in a strategic planning process that culminates in a document that goes to our Academic Senate for endorsement. And then that is followed by an implementation period for the next three or four years, and there's a committee that has the membership of all the major campus stakeholders. They are responsible for monitoring the implementation of the plan. And it has served us very well and I think people on the campus would acknowledge that it's an effective process that helps the campus to chart its future and direction.

Over time the successive plans build on each other, each cycle helping to operationalize and implement goals laid forth in the previous one. For example, Welty explained:

> The first plan was fairly aspirational in the sense that it made the most statements about things that we were going to try to accomplish. It wasn't until some of those aspirations were modified in the second process that we really achieved some of the goals. Now, interestingly enough, because we were pretty successful in the second planning process, people's sights are elevated and they are looking to kind of go to the next level as an institution, I think. So I think each process has been a little bit different but it served us very well in terms of building on what happened previously.

CSU San Francisco is currently in Phase 2 of a strategic planning process that began in the late 1990s. Like CSU Fresno's process, the two stages built on each other considerably. In Phase 1, the Commission chose "all-encompassing, blue-sky" themes such as internationalization, diversity, user-friendliness and community service. "Stuff like, if someone came along tomorrow and gave me $50 million dollars, what would we wish for," President Corrigan said. Over 156 recommendations were developed, few of which were implemented. In Phase 2, the Commission is focusing on more "practical" themes such as the academic experience, the student experience, the employee experience, and the university vis-à-vis the environment. Moreover, Phase 2 of the strategic planning process would place far greater emphasis on prioritizing the initiatives to help them be implemented. Corrigan explained:

> In Phase 1 we paid too much attention on coming up with recommendations, and had far too many of them. We did not pay sufficient attention to developing a realistic implementation strategy and assessment plan. This time around we made it clear to the Commission from the very beginning that every recommendation that is put on the table has to have an implementation plan and an assessment strategy, as well as an indication of cost factors. So we've learned a tremendous amount about the need to tie recommendations to assessment plans and implementation strategies, right from the get-go, rather than to assume that they're going to occur at the back end, if you will.

Waiting for the Right Time to Begin Strategic Planning

Interestingly, some presidents arrive at a campus only to decide that the present is *not* the best time to embark on a strategic planning process. Instead, they wait for a better opportunity, or engage in a scaled-back version to keep the campus moving forward. For example, when Bob Caret arrived at San Jose State in 1995, the campus was still "reeling" from a rushed, top-down strategic planning process that had been hastily conducted to meet the requirements of a pending WASC reaccreditation effort. As a result, he decided that the present time was not the wisest to embark on a formal strategic planning process. He said:

> [The previous effort] was put together very quickly and without much collaboration and dialogue. As a result, the campus was in no mood to go through that kind of process. They were much more concerned with the fundamental day-to-day life at the moment.

Instead, he decided to focus on four key ideas that had already been discussed as part of the previous effort: Enrollment Management, Student Success, Campus Climate, and Information Literacy/Technology. These were the issues he focused on for the next few years. He explained:

> When I first came [to San Jose State] and put together the compilation of goals that came out of previous efforts, I had really four primary subthemes [Enrollment Management, Student Success, Campus Climate, and Information Literacy/Technology] that we were working on, and you could say those four subthemes quickly over and over again. If I was in a town meeting at a college, or if I was meeting with managers, or with a student group at a study break, I could use those four themes and they would be reported to the press. I can't say that everybody in the campus would repeat them but I bet you, many of them would know them at this point.

Six years later Caret concluded that the campus had focused on "pressing issues" for long enough and that it was time to devote attention to the campus's future, or "next steps." He and his staff decided to launch a more strategic planning formal effort that will not be completed until 2007. The aim is for the plan to coincide with the campus's 150th birthday, which will occur that same year.

As at San Jose State, Chico State President Esteban arrived at a campus that was in a difficult situation. The year was 1993. Esteban explained that the campus had gone through very serious budget cuts, and enrollment had been reduced significantly. The previous president had tried to eliminate an entire college, and the relationship between the university and the community was at a low point. Rather than embark on an entirely new strategic planning effort, Esteban decided to pull together what had been done from the existing plan. This required consolidating individual colleges' strategic plans and ironing out inconsistencies. Esteban explained:

When I came it was clear that this was going to be a much tougher job than I had anticipated. Also, I saw that each college had put together a strategic plan, and realized that there were a lot of things that were contradictory in that it didn't seem as though it was possible to do one thing in one college and something totally opposite in another. So I decided to put together a group of people that included faculty, staff, students, community leaders, alumni, and basically told them to consider all the realities that existed in terms of the budget, and to come up with a plan that would allow the university to move forward.

To help implement the plan, he gave it to Academic Affairs and to the new provost and the deans, and said, "Take this document and steal from it what is the most significant, and that we will have a strategic plan for the university, and then we'll move forward."

Tailoring the Strategic Planning Process to the President's Initiatives

In many cases the strategic planning process was viewed by presidents as a means to an ends, or as a way to achieve other goals. For example, at CSU San Francisco, Phase 1 of the strategic planning process was highly instrumental in helping the campus gain reaccreditation from WASC. Specifically, the campus was allowed to fulfill self-study requirements of the WASC reaccreditation process by reviewing the results of their strategic planning process. CSU San Francisco President Corrigan explained:

We had the opportunity, with our lost accreditation, to review the results of our strategic planning as our self-study—that is, how well had we been able to carry forward, to carry through on the goals that we'd set for ourselves. Where had we handled these well? Where had we not? What had we left out? WASC came in, and we went through the accreditation process with flying colors.

At Cal Poly San Luis Obispo, the strategic planning was used to help revise the campus's master plan and garner necessary resources to grow the campus. President Baker explained the intersection:

The strategic planning process was absolutely crucial to the master plan. . . . Indeed, the physical master plan of the campus came after and derived directly from the strategic planning process. A year ago last March we presented the master plan revision to the Board of Trustees. Now we're implementing that master plan, which considers expansion of some programs, maintenance of other programs at some level, identification of new areas that we will pursue, and of course, specification of the required physical and financial resources.

After the master plan was approved, President Baker used the strategic planning process as a means to raise resources for the laboratory-intensive courses offered at the campus, at a time when the state's money was running out. Advice on how to raise resources was obtained from an advisory board comprised of company CEOs. Baker explained:

> Two-thirds of our students are in laboratory-intensive programs that the state doesn't fully pay for. You can't just overcome this financial challenge by economies of scale—if you're losing money on each student, you can't make it up by having more students. But through the strategic planning process, we were able to get a lot of advice—primarily from the business community—related to how we were going to achieve resources to pay for our programs. This led to our three-pronged plan to support our programs: pursuing a program cost differential with the system and state, developing a fee partnership with our students, and setting goals for targeted private fund-raising.

San Jose State's president used a modified strategic planning process to move his campus toward what he called the "Metropolitan University"—an umbrella concept that included the four subthemes but also differentiated the campus from other universities. President Caret explained:

> I came in and basically defined the campus as a Metropolitan University of Silicon Valley. They had never heard the term Metropolitan University . . . a comprehensive campus that happens to be in a metropolitan region. We were talking about a way to delineate ourselves in contrast to, for example, Stanford, Berkeley, or Santa Clara University. And as we began to debate, people realized we weren't going to try and convert the school into a vocational school. The notion of a Metropolitan University began to take on form, and today pretty much everybody calls us the Metropolitan University of Silicon Valley. That's a very simple way to talk about this very large, old, vibrant, and complex university. And then we have the four subthemes that really gave us a day-to-day focus, even though we were doing lots of things under those themes.

The Role of Leadership

The fact that most campuses follow a highly participative approach does not negate the need for leadership, according to presidents. This is especially true in situations that demand quick decisions, or those that don't allow for extensive dialogue. An example of such an issue is a budgetary decision. San Jose State's Bob Caret explained:

> With budgets, we've always tried to involve people in dialogue. But the budget is always changing, day-to-day sometimes. So you can't just call together a committee every day when you're making a very quick decision. Sometimes it's just a "yes/no" on the phone, so you have to have the ability as a leader to determine when you need dialogue and when it's right for you to make that decision and just inform people. So I think [strategic planning] does require formal leadership and not just management. It needs people who can make decisions.

Another aspect of leadership is keeping the vision associated with a strategic plan alive. Sonoma State President Arminana does this by repeating themes over and over to his campus constituents:

> I say our themes over and over and over. I say, retention, graduation, satisfaction to somebody, every day. And if I haven't said that I'm going to have to go and face my dog and tell him those three words! I also repeat those themes more formally, through two speeches that I give every year at convocation to the faculty, staff, students, and community. So I continue to push that vision and elaborate on it.

CSU Chico President Esteban also keeps the vision alive by demonstrating that the goals contained in a strategic plan are actually followed:

> It is very important that you demonstrate to people that the decisions you're making are consistent with the strategic plan. For instance, after five years of having a strategic plan, at my convocation speech, I went over it again. I took each one of the five strategic priorities, and I said what we had accomplished within each one of them. I gave specific examples, because in the last five years we had had a lot of new faculty, and a lot of new staff, and I wasn't sure that people were as aware as they ought to be (1) that we had a strategic plan, (2) that it had been very successful, and (3) that we needed to continue to work within it in order to continue to have successes. And by demonstrating the successes that we had accumulated, I think that it made that a living document.

Yet another element of leadership is "walking the talk," or putting the espoused concepts into practice. One president who literally does this is Sonoma State President Arminana:

When you see the president bending over and picking up garbage, then others do it. That denotes a university that is active, organized, disciplined, and prompt! That is very hard to plan. If you put in a plan, that everyone should bend over and pick up that piece of paper, it means very little. It is hard to articulate in a plan. It won't get done. It has to become part of the behavior, the thinking process. But if you model it, it becomes what people do—even students. That is part of our philosophy.

Implementation

A final theme highlighted by presidents was the importance of implementation. CSU Chico President Esteban explained: "Once you have the plan in place, it has to be implementable. I mean, if you cannot implement, if it's either too dreamy, too overwhelming, too visionary, even though it's good, you're not going to have successes." As noted earlier, one strategy to improve the odds of implementation is to follow a participatory approach. Another is to make sure that the desired new behaviors are supported by the proper rewards and incentives. Esteban explained:

Once you have that strategic plan, then you have to ensure that the rewards and the incentives are such that they are consistent with those priorities, because if faculty, staff, and everybody else perceives that there is a disconnect between what you claim that you're trying to do and what you actually do, then the whole thing falls apart.

For plans to be implemented, they must be closely tied to the university budget. That is, unless resources are made available to implement the recommendations, presidents warned, they will die. At CSU Fullerton the goals were emphasized to the point that plans and budgets were built around them. President Gordon explained:

It's one of the most important actions that I've been involved with here at the campus. As I say, it's universally used. People know the goals and the number of them almost by rote. When they send proposals forward they refer directly to planning goal or goals 1, 2, 3, 4, and they build the proposal actually around that goal or goals. The process also drives budget decisions. So I feel, and we actually set up on an annual basis, budgeting based on request under certain kinds of request, using this process.

CSU Chico President Esteban explained how even faculty now understand the need to align with the plan to obtain resources:

And although people did not believe that we were going to stick by the strategic plan, it has become a document that is accepted by everyone. Everybody knows that in order to get some of the resources that we have put aside to implement these [strategic decisions], they have to be tied to the plan. Even now, when faculty prepare their documents for promotion and tenure, they try to show how what they do is part and parcel of what the university is attempting to do.

A formal way to tie the strategic plan to the budget is to implement performance-based budgeting. Esteban explained how it works, and how each college's performance is evaluated:

We implemented performance-based budgeting. Before, money was allocated on a historical basis. We said, if we continued to do this, frankly, nobody makes any decisions, because it's just historical. And historical doesn't necessarily mean that the decisions that were made at the beginning were the right decisions. So we agreed that everybody would get a base budget. We then set aside a significant amount of money that we allocated to colleges on a performance basis. So, for instance, every year colleges ask the provost for certain monies to accomplish certain goals and of course those goals have to fit within the general strategic plan. And then we allocate the resources accordingly. To judge the performance of the colleges, at the beginning of each year (or at the end of the year), the provost meets with every dean and asks him or her to detail the achievements of the preceding year, and then indicate what they will be working on. And then the provost and I—mostly the provost—really, will look at that and see what they've done, and then on the basis of what they've done, then we allocate the resources for the following year.

At times, resource constraints make the attainment of strategic goals simply impossible. CSU Los Angeles President Rosser provided an example of when he had to postpone the building of a fine arts complex:

There was one campus goal in particular that was deferred for a period of time. It involved the final component of the Luckman Fine Arts Complex. We had to defer that project because of the financial climate. [Now, however] it is currently nearing completion.

— 5 —

When Sectors Collide

In the first chapter, which was based on a review of key thought leaders, we offered a broad perspective on the contemporary organizational environment, emphasizing the need to (1) accept the increasing pace of change and the accompanying impact on organizational effectiveness, (2) redesign organizations to welcome complexity and turbulence as the new, conventional normalcy, (3) recognize that an organization's external environment can have a differential effect on individuals within the organization, and (4) assess the appropriateness of current step-by-step, structured approaches to strategy formulation and to consider a more amorphous, spontaneous set of actions and decisions under the rubric of strategic thinking. Moreover, we postulated that these ideas were common to all organizations, regardless of sector. Yet, as we began our interviews of leaders within Hewlett-Packard, Los Angeles County, and the California State University, these conclusions felt incorrect, even counterintuitive! Simply stated, we grappled with questions such as, could the external environment of a municipal government or a university system really be as turbulent as a high-tech firm? Could organizations in different sectors adopt similar designs and approaches to strategic issues? Could the dynamics of strategic thinking actually mean the same in each sector? To answer these questions and others, we proposed three sets of questions:

1. How do senior managers characterize their environment in terms of both the pace of change and strategic issues? What are the sources of environmental uncertainty and/or disorder?
2. How do senior managers approach the strategy making process? What specific role(s) do senior managers play in the strategy making process? Can we ascertain the thought processes used by senior managers to determine strategies?

Figure 5.1 **Levels of Analysis**

External Voice
(the literature)

Leaders'
Voices

Our
Voice

3. Can the characteristics of an emergent model of strategy making be identified?

In the earlier chapters, we offered two sets of voices: (1) external, mostly from academe, providing the theoretical understanding of the differences in both organizational environments and approaches to strategy making, and (2) internal leaders, from three giant organizations representing different sectors, reflecting on their specific environmental milieu and involvement in strategy making activities. In this chapter, as depicted in Figure 5.1, we add our voice, providing a personal interpretation of the collective interview data.

The Eye of the Beholder

In assessing the "lightning bolts"—significant external forces that organizations must assess and respond to—as expected, our three giants had several major areas of differentiation from each other (i.e., globalization and growth through acquisition for Hewlett-Packard; federal and state rules and regulations, the Board of Supervisors, and media for Los Angeles County; and housing costs for the California State University). More frequent, however, as shown in Table 5.1, was the overlapping commonality of forces between these organizations. Below, we take a close look at these shared forces.

The Economy Is Causing Anxiety in All Three Organizations

When asked to identify the external forces influencing their organization, regardless of sector, over 60 percent of the leaders initially responded that the

Table 5.1

Forces Affecting Each Organization

Force	H-P	LAC	CSU
Economy	✓	✓	✓
Technology	✓	✓	✓
Customer demands	✓	✓	
Geopolitical situation	✓	✓	
Competition	✓		✓
Globalization	✓		
Demographics		✓	✓
Public accountability		✓	✓
Rules and regulations		✓	
The board		✓	
The media		✓	
Housing costs			✓

ongoing economic recession was the single most dominating concern driving the larger organization and their specific organizational unit or area of accountability. In listening to these leaders, we heard a sense of foreboding; that is, unless the economy improved soon, major organizational disruptions would occur. However, the perceived consequences differed. At H-P the economy was a "survival-type" concern. The global situation was deemed a worldwide slowdown, causing reduced spending in the IT industry, a situation that was exacerbated by disproportionately high corporate IT spending during the late 1990s and the failure of these IT investments to attain the expected benefits. Faced with only minimum signs of an economic uptick and a saturated IT market, H-P interviewees struggled to identify potential growth markets and even to forecast quarterly performance. Several feared for the long-term existence of their business unit or group and, therefore, adopted a short-term mentality.

For both the CSU and County, where there was no threat to continued existence or demand for services, the concern over the weak economy was 180 degrees different. Due to California's weak economy and unpredictable financial future, leaders lamented the necessity of budget reductions and the accompanying decrease in services for needy populations. Over and over, we heard how the loss of revenue would deprive County residents of health, mental health, and social services or reduce library hours and park programs. For the CSU, the economic situation meant that the system's growth would be curtailed, that instructional quality would be compromised by increased class size, and that investments in student services such as counselors would suffer. Moreover, the campus shortfalls placed pressure on the presidents to engage in fund-raising, which was difficult, since it required a cultural shift for both the system and most campuses.

Technological Change Is Pressuring All Three Organizations

Similarly, although many of our leaders identified the "technology revolution" as a substantive and continuous driving force, again, their perspectives diverged. At H-P the key, complex question was how to sustain its historical role as the driver of technological innovation and simultaneously respond to technological discontinuities as they occurred for continued survival. This reflected a world that was becoming more digitized and where technology was ubiquitous for both business and personal use. Simply stated, H-P had to contend simultaneously with increasing customer expectations and unexpected technological advances by both competitors and partners.

For the County the technological revolution presented a slightly different dilemma. Like H-P, they had to cope with the pressure of increasing public demands for interactive access to government services, but unlike H-P, they had to accept the fact that adequate investment resources for technology would never exist. That is, the types of technological applications desired were, for the most part, too costly. As noted in chapter 3, this was a continuously changing balancing act. Ironically, then, the same residents desired increased interaction with government through technology, but were not willing to incur the accompanying expense. The inability to secure new systems and applications was also creating internal frustration as labor-intensive record keeping in areas such as finance and human resources became antiquated and opportunities to acquire new, automated systems proved overly costly.

Unlike both H-P and the County, the CSU leaders were generally pleased with the system's response to the technology explosion. Under Cornerstones, the CSU established the adoption of technology as an internal imperative—mainly, attaining systemwide administrative alignment across campuses and the integration of the Internet into classrooms and other student and faculty activities on each campus. At the time of the interviews, the CSU was integrating massive data systems (e.g., PeopleSoft) and campuses were providing incentives to faculty to develop courses for delivery over the Web. In short, unlike the other two giants, the leaders of the CSU felt comfortable with their ability to handle the technological force.

Customer Demand Confronts Both Hewlett-Packard and Los Angeles County

Inextricably linked to the technology force, as noted above, is the customer. At H-P this represented a continuation of its customer-centric approach to the marketplace. The Total Customer Experience (TCE) became a mantra for the new H-P, postmerger. Leaders were clear that at all levels of customer, from families purchasing home computers to enterprises acquiring complex systems and services, the increasingly sophisticated customer could demand that (1) their requirements be paramount in the design of future products and services, and (2) a satisfying " buying experience" should exist at all levels of the buying spectrum. It was clear to us that in the competitiveness of a saturated, rapidly changing market, the customer's desires ruled.

For County leaders, there was a realization that residents were increasingly demanding a shift from the industrial-era methods for doing business to a new information age approach. For these leaders, this represented a dramatic change and an uncertain path. We often sensed that these leaders, similar to H-P, were seeking new ways to engage their constituents.

The Current Geopolitical Situation Creates Unexpected Uncertainty for Hewlett-Packard and Los Angeles County

For both Hewlett-Packard and Los Angeles County, the events of 9/11 added a new external force to an already changing environment. As a global company, operating in 178 countries, H-P had to increase its investment in both plant and employee security worldwide. Similarly, under the auspices of Homeland Security, the County had to establish new working relationships among its public safety departments and among its departments and federal and other municipal governments. Like H-P, this required a considerable reallocation of funds.

H-P also had to adjust to the continually expanding global marketplace. As our leaders indicated, as emerging countries became more developed and connected, they placed more and more demands (as customers) on H-P and its competitors. Not only did these countries focus on technology products and services, they also required H-P to be a good corporate citizen. For H-P, this meant that leaders had to both scan more effectively to understand the unique characteristics of different cultures and increase the agility of their units to respond to global shifts in real time.

Demographic Shifts Affect Los Angeles County and the California State University System

For Los Angeles County, the changes in population characteristics seemed to impinge on every aspect of organizational life. The continuous increase in demand for mandated services combined with the identification of unique ethnic community requirements (e.g., specific health issues, language barriers) seemed unrelenting. Our leaders appeared "pained" by their inability to

do more. Simultaneously, several leaders worried about the County's ability to maintain a highly qualified, diverse workforce, a situation exacerbated by the exodus of long-term employees and the inability to compete with the private sector for today's new knowledge workers.

At the CSU, demographics were an ever-present, but slow moving major force. Our leaders readily acknowledged that Tidal Wave II would severely strain the system, making it difficult for the CSU to accomplish its mission of ensuring access to all eligible high school graduates, yet there seemed to be an inherent belief that incremental progress was occurring and that this issue was resolvable. Several of our leaders thought there would be increased pressure for the hiring of a more diverse workforce, given the growing ethnic diversity of the CSU student body. Thus, although for different reasons, both the CSU and the County had similar hiring challenges.

Public Accountability Pressures Increase for Both Los Angeles County and the California State University System

For both the County and the California State University system, as public entities, external oversight and demands for demonstrable program and service outcomes are constants. Leaders of both, however, perceived increased scrutiny of their operations. For the County, it surfaced through additional laws and regulations that required further procedural compliance and limited managerial discretion in deciding how best to meet local municipal needs. There was a belief that federal and state lawmakers and regulators were intruding into local prerogatives.

The CSU leaders viewed the same force somewhat differently. For them, there was increasing public intolerance for the operational outcomes, such as low graduation rates and the lengthy time to graduation that were creating pressure. As these concerns mounted, public lawmakers were starting to require more answers and more overt activities to rectify the situation. Our interviewees were wary, however, believing that increased state oversight and required accountability-related activities would lead to great CSU bureaucratization, hamper innovation at the campus level, and overburden already busy faculty.

Competition Sizzles at Hewlett-Packard and Begins to Emerge at the California State University

Since H-P operates as a private enterprise in a free market economy, major forces at work include the actions of competitors, the accompanying impact of competitive action(s) on costs, and the role of commoditization. Our leaders highlighted the constant need to differentiate products to win customers, develop unique and/or proprietary products, and reduce costs. A basic underlying message was that in the electronics industry, there are no comfortable periods for companies to glide through the sales cycles with undifferentiated products.

Competition was a questionable, although clearly identified, force at the CSU. Opinions differed on the threat level posed by the rapid growth of private, for-profit educational institutions such as Phoenix and DeVry. Some presidents worried that these institutions could challenge state universities nationwide, citing superior performance in areas such as class scheduling, time-to-degree, and career services. Others, mainly central administrators, envisioned little threat, noting that the current model would continue because of the high demand imposed by Tidal Wave II.

An Absolutist Versus Relativist View of Turbulence

Taken together, the absolute number and heterogeneity of forces impacting each organization (i.e., environmental complexity) and the variation in the ability of our leaders to predict both the actual direction and rate of change (i.e., dynamism) certainly supported the conclusion of significant cross-sector environmental turbulence. Moreover, as expressed by our leaders but often absent in the macro-level analysis described by observers, were the interdependencies among these forces, such as the customer demand-technology or economy-demographic connections, making the cumulative influence of these forces even more difficult to interpret.

In an effort to understand these forces more clearly, we extrapolated from the comments of our leaders their perceptions regarding the dynamism of their environment. As summarized in Table 5.2, by categorizing the forces by unpredictability and speed of the force, a more robust picture emerged. Whereas Los Angeles County had the most complex environment (i.e., absolute number of forces), H-P experienced the greatest uncertainty with three forces classified as unpredictable and rapidly changing (technology, competition, globalization) and the remainder either unpredictable or rapidly changing. This represented a very conventional high-tech environment, for which H-P must continually maintain focus.

Los Angeles County, on the other hand, had only one force—federal and state rules and regulations—that appeared both unpredictable and rapidly changing, while every other force was either unpredictable or rapidly changing. This was a picture of turbulence that has rarely been associated with government. It negated the notion that government leaders have an easier job of managing their environment. In fact, it is at the California State University

Table 5.2

Forces Affecting Each Organization by Speed and Unpredictability

Force	H-P	LAC	CSU
Economy	(unpredictable)	(unpredictable)	(unpredictable)
Technology	(both)	(rapid)	(rapid)
Customer demands	(rapid)	(rapid)	
Geopolitical situation	(unpredictable)	(unpredictable)	
Competition	(both)		(force)
Globalization	(both)		
Demographics		(rapid)	(force)
Public accountability		(rapid)	(force)
Rules and regulations		(both)	
The board		(unpredictable)	
The media		(unpredictable)	
Housing costs			(force)

Key: (unpredictable icon) = force is unpredictable.

(rapid icon) = force changes rapidly.

(both icon) = force is both unpredictable and rapidly changing.

(force icon) = a force, but not particularly unpredictable or rapidly changing.

system that the forces seemed "under control," with four of the six forces not particularly unpredictable or rapidly changing.

The above assessment denotes an absolutist view of the environment, that is, a straightforward assessment of the environmental forces affecting an organization at a point in time. It focuses on the environment-organization interaction—number, unpredictability, and speed of forces affecting the organization. Our leaders' comments, however, overwhelmingly suggested to us that both environmental complexity and dynamism needed to be filtered through an individual lens, creating a relativist view. We concluded that (1) even if the environment stayed both complex and dynamic for an extended

Figure 5.2   **Organizational Turbulence: Past and Present**

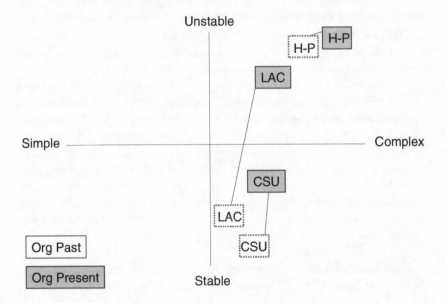

period of time, individuals functioning in that environment might become desensitized and recalibrate their assessment scale from very high initial turbulence to low turbulence, and (2) organizational movement from one type of environment to another environment creates its own turbulence. Thus, at Hewlett-Packard, nearly all the leaders described the environmental pace of change as constant; although from an absolutist perspective, it was organizationally the most dynamic. We postulated that this reflected a multi-decade experience in this type of private-sector environment. At Los Angeles County, however, where the environmental forces were basically simple and easily accommodated for long periods of time, the increased complexity meant leaders had to alter their behavior significantly. From this (pictured in Figure 5.2), we postulate that the pace of change at the individual level is much more dramatic for the County leaders relative to Hewlett-Packard leaders, although the latter operate in a more uncertain environment.

Closing Thoughts I

As these leaders described the major external forces affecting their organizations, we found ourselves contemplating longer-term meanings. Below we discuss three possibilities that we found most intriguing.

First, as discussed in chapter 1 and clearly indicated by the leaders in all three sectors, one of the central challenges for today's organizational leaders is to understand the potential impact of the technological revolution and to position their organization or unit to meet anticipated customer demands. During the past ten years, for instance, the global use of computers has doubled and use of the Internet continues to increase exponentially. Indeed there seems to be a consensus that IT (and technology generally) is still in the early stages of development and that its overall impact is still highly undetermined. For example, we were reminded of the 1978 comment by Kenneth Olson, founder and CEO of Digital Equipment Corporation, that there was no need for any individual to have a computer in their home, or the prediction in the early 1990s that it would require 20 to 30 years to map the human genome. More recently, who would have speculated that small, private entrepreneurial firms such as SpaceShipOne, which were not part of the aerospace establishment, would successfully go into space and potentially create a new industry for civilian space travel? In each instance the advances in technology far exceeded conventional thought.

It seemed to us that, overwhelmingly, these leaders assumed that future "winners and losers" would be determined almost exclusively by technological competitiveness. Unlike the economy, which represented a cyclical force, we detected an acceptance—albeit reluctant, except for a few H-P leaders—that the technology pressure would remain constant. In short, the pace of technological change appeared to represent a force of nature or a tectonic shift whose impact would not be fully understood for many generations.

From our perspective, for instance, the merger between Hewlett-Packard and Compaq Computer represented a potential beginning to more high-tech industry mergers and takeovers. We could envision an era where customer expectations continued to increase significantly, the cost of research and development investments in new products became insupportable to investors, and the business focus shifted to "buying" market share and/or product niches. Like the banking industry, the small would disappear and a few large competitors would remain. In fact, several of the H-P leaders questioned whether H-P or any high-tech firms could continually reinvent itself. Thus, while our H-P leaders believed that an economic turnaround would restore the current sluggish industry health, several also noted that customers were still not experiencing a substantial enough return on previous investments during the 1990s and that recovery would be very slow. We wondered, on the other hand, if an economic turnaround would also exacerbate a possible industry "shakeout."

While many people in government, as expressed by Los Angeles County leaders, recognized the need to move from an industrial-era method for doing business to a new information approach, the path did not seem very clear. From our perspective, we could not imagine many municipalities maintaining the capability of meeting citizens' demands through new or even updated technology—it is too costly. Even today, many government agencies have a five- to seven-year cycle for obtaining either new computers or approval for new systems. For example, we are aware of several large agencies and municipalities that only recently obtained email access for all their workers. A more likely scenario, we believe, envisions the outsourcing of most IT services, including a renewed emphasis on contracting out internal support services such as human resources. Thus government would become more involved in contract management than in the direct delivery of services. In short, we suggest the continued expansion of the market for providing services to government, so that government can better serve citizens.

For higher education, where the Tidal Wave II era guarantees a constant supply of students (i.e., customers), technology may still cause some disorder in the marketplace. Specifically, we see the steady growth in online learning as an emergent product, early in its life cycle. We wonder if those universities and colleges best able to offer online courses can attract students from many countries—thus contributing to global understanding—might attain a competitive advantage. Additionally, we see the more elite universities, particularly those with large endowments, investing heavily in technology, so they can deliver interactive programs worldwide from their core campuses. Overseas students in developing countries may be able to stay at home and get a degree from an Ivy League university. Besides this obvious competitiveness between the elites, the expansion of technology into the classroom may further increase the disparity between the elites and the state-supported universities.

Second, in our initial discussion of these leaders' descriptions of the external forces affecting their organizations, we found ourselves speculating on the degree to which external forces interacted with each other, knowing that the greater the interaction between external forces, the greater the environmental complexity and turbulence. That is, when forces are interdependent, when one force shifts, all connected forces tend to move, thereby increasing the overall impact. Conversely, when forces are largely independent of each other, movement by one force may not affect others significantly.

Although we did not formally analyze the interaction between the environmental forces in each organization, several leaders did highlight some of the interdependencies. For example, at Hewlett-Packard, as noted above, the economy directly influenced customers' spending decisions and, consequently, could impact both H-P's global efforts and research and development investments. In Los Angeles County the changing demographics and

accompanying health and social population needs have resulted in new leg-
islatively imposed mandates, progressively affected program resource allocations, and provided new media focus on County government's shortcomings.
Similarly, the CSU, albeit more in control of its destiny, found the Tidal
Wave II influx closely related to public accountability, due to campus space
needs, course availability, and graduation rates, as well as the inability to
attract new out-of-state faculty because of high housing costs.

For us, this interactive dimension also highlighted the need for both active
learning by organizational leaders and increased focus on the adaptive capacity of organizations. That is, given the complexity caused by this
interactivity among external forces, leaders must give up the notion that they
can create stability and become comfortable with constant ambiguity. This
means that leaders will be continuously analyzing their environment, reaching conclusions and making decisions with minimal information, and learning from the outcomes, thereby beginning the process again. Also, this requires
systems thinking in order to anticipate the potential "domino effect" of an
external change. At the macro level, the organization must design itself to
respond faster to the daily learning.

Third, we found ourselves joining the "chorus of observers" questioning
the instructional orientation adopted for most graduate-level strategy courses
offered by business schools.[1] From our viewpoint, utilizing both readings
and cases, the current approach emphasizes the importance of strategy formulation, while virtually ignoring the dynamic environment impacting the
execution of the strategy. Thus, strategy courses focus almost exclusively on
the "up-front" analysis of the environment, the identification of market factors, and the means to obtain product differentiation and competitive advantage. Often the class discussions seek to identify all possible factors that
need to be considered when developing a strategic plan. It is evident to us, as
increasingly noted by observers of business education, that this approach
reinforces the belief that once all factors are identified, a leader can systematically implement the strategy. Such thinking represents a more stable era
and we imagine it misleads students.

We do believe, however, that a sound assessment of the current situation
is necessary; we just don't find it sufficient. Omitted from the current strategy courses are the behavioral skills needed to adapt to changing external
conditions, as so often described by the leaders in this study. Indeed, implicit in the responses of many of our leaders was the acceptance that the
day you make a strategic choice, you do not know the outcome. It is a
commitment to put thought and resources into achieving the intended outcome and an understanding that you must be capable of dealing with the
effects of a changing environment and the accompanying impact on your

strategy. This may include taking new, immediate action to sustain your strategy or even a determination that a shift in strategic direction is necessary. For us, extrapolating from our leaders' comments, the key questions become how do you prepare students for this challenge? How do you increase the adaptive capacity of the individual to handle the unknowable? Briefly, we suggest that the graduate strategy course include (1) scenario development techniques to encourage consideration of a wider range of strategic choices by shifting assumptions about external and internal conditions; (2) computer-based simulations to provide prompt feedback on decisions and thereby require action learning and possible modification of previous decisions; (3) debates to "force" students to defend alternative strategies using the same set of data; and (4) living cases where external leaders present actual situations and students must ask critical questions to explore possible strategic choices. The goal is to add complexity anchored in reality to the study of strategy formulation and execution.

In the End, It Is a Balancing Act

When asked to describe the primary purpose of strategic planning within their respective organizations, these leaders offered three very different frameworks. At Hewlett-Packard, strategic planning was predominately a road map for "survival and growth" in a hostile environment. As some H-P leaders noted, a dual urgency existed within H-P. First, the company has been concerned with global demands all the time, as it has sought to understand the many, highly differentiated markets. Second, the company has felt increased pressure to develop new products and services at a faster pace, as it has responded to the challenge of product commoditization. At Los Angeles County, strategic planning was a means to align silos and promote interdepartmental cooperation. The Guiding Coalition acted as an executive team through consensus decision-making. At the California State University, Cornerstones, the official strategic plan, served as a touchstone for campus presidents. Basically the presidents had free reign in deciding how they would align with Cornerstones and nearly total freedom in setting the direction for their campus.

Yet, when asked about the structure of strategic planning in their respective organizations, the leaders in this study depicted a bifurcated process. In all three organizations, there existed both a highly structured, centrally controlled plan that placed differentiated performance demands and alignment requirements on organizational units, while simultaneously allowing leaders varying degrees of discretion in determining their specific unit strategies. Not surprisingly, the formal position of the leader, either as the head of a central staff organization or line organization, affected their perception of the relationship between the organizational and unit levels.

At H-P the leaders discussed strategy from three vantage points: corporate strategy, strategic management, and strategy formulation. Both the executive vice presidents and senior vice presidents, who participated on the Executive Committee, described corporate strategy as a series of shared decisions about developing new products and services and entering new markets. Within this executive group, there was a strong emphasis on both comprehending the potential impact of key external forces and obtaining competitive intelligence. This was continually framed by conversations aimed at understanding shareholder perceptions and establishing line unit accountability in meeting performance targets. According to several of the operational leaders in this study, this frequently produced a short-term mentality (i.e., the overwhelming importance of quarterly numbers for the investment community) that they had to balance against day-to-day strategic management decisions and actions needed to meet their unit's specific customer requirements. Several of these line leaders noted that corporate-operational clashes were not unusual, but that access to the executive team tended to resolve differences quickly. This was a significant improvement over the old decentralized structure where few mechanisms existed to ameliorate differences.

The formal linkage between executive leadership and line leaders occurred in the strategy formulation process where formal assessments of products, services, and markets plus leadership performance occurred. Although the particular approach changed over time, from Ten-Step Planning to Strategic Planning and Review (SpaR), the mechanics stayed relatively constant; it was a very deliberate process for analyzing data and arriving at rational decisions. Given this measured approach, several leaders mentioned the need for scenario thinking, including constant scanning, adjusting, recommitting— all requiring flexibility—to defend or change their focus. We concluded that while the strategic planning process remained highly deliberate, despite the environmental turbulence, the day-to-day execution was becoming more and more tactical, as leaders tried to meet the short-term goals.

What did seem to change, however, was the increased internal "churn and uncertainty" caused by the merger with Compaq, which virtually doubled the company size. Often mentioned by the H-P leaders were the added pressures associated with (1) integrating two very different companies and managing the internal dynamics, including the need to gain horizontal alignment for critical strategic decisions, (2) showing short-term gains through increased efficiencies and product and marketplace growth, and (3) doubting personal survival in a redesigned organization. A few leaders confided that they were not sure that they wanted to continue the "juggling act" much longer. One operational leader seemed to sum up many opinions, when he noted that he missed the old H-P, where he truly controlled his own destiny. Now he had to "manage" corporate and customer demands simultaneously, even when they did not seem compatible.

In listening to the H-P leaders, we were surprised by the apparent disconnect between their environment and the strategy formulation process. Given the external and internal turbulence, we had assumed that we would observe a more organic strategic planning process. Rather, the actual strategic process remained quite deliberate. And the new operational strategists seemed to be driven more by immediacies than longer-term vision.

Los Angeles County, prior to the development of the current strategic plan and the formation of the Guiding Coalition to oversee implementation, reminded us of a "holding company," similar to Hewlett-Packard's product divisions before the arrival of Carly Fiorina. That is, metaphorically the County "owned" each of the 37 departments, and the Board of Supervisors established core policies for all, but primarily let them operate and be judged independently of each other. Unanimously, the County leaders in this study agreed that the chief administrative officer had created a sense of unity and cross-departmental collaboration by gaining agreement on goals for the common good. It was apparent to us, however, that the administrative leaders spoke with greater emotional enthusiasm than the operational leaders. This seemed natural, since the initial focus of the strategic plan was on organizational areas such as workforce excellence, organizational effectiveness, and fiscal responsibility. Thus, for these administrative leaders, the strategic plan became a tool for promulgating new programs and practices Countywide (e.g., establish framework for a performance measurement system; design and implement a common systems architecture for Countywide administrative systems; implement plan to preserve and protect the County's critical infrastructure). As one leader indicated, the strategic plan represented the means and the Guiding Coalition the forum for leveraging administrative changes through the County.

Unlike the administrative leaders, the line department leaders were more restrained when describing their thoughts about strategic planning. This was due primarily to three factors: (1) they pictured strategic planning with its focus on collaboration and teamwork as being driven by one individual, the CAO, and therefore wondered if it too would disappear at some point—although they hoped not; (2) even after adopting the strategic plan, the Board of Supervisors rarely paid attention to its major initiatives—the Board remained focused on the individual departments; and (3) unlike the administrative departments who could drive their major initiatives through the County strategic plan, their major departmental programs took place at the "local" level; therefore, these leaders understand that government organizations needed to become more customer-centered and that regardless of the success of the County strategic plan, they would still be evaluated by their department's performance.

As we listened to these leaders' voices, we kept returning to the role of the Guiding Coalition (CG) as the primary mechanism for overseeing implementation of the strategic plan. The GC was a prominent theme in nearly all the interviews. For us, the GC represented a typical collateral organizational structure, that is, a parallel structure designed to augment the formal organization by providing an alternative setting and accompanying resources to resolve substantive matters outside the rules of the bureaucracy. We wondered if the GC could become an institutionalized element of County governance. At the time of the study, it wasn't apparent, yet the County leaders implied that without the GC, strategic planning would again become marginalized.

Not surprisingly, within the California State University system, the collegial model of higher education dominated the approach to strategy formulation and execution. That is, at both the CSU and campus level, virtually all leaders employed a participative approach that entailed obtaining broad participation from constituencies to gain "buy-in" and involvement in all aspects of the strategic planning process. The development of Cornerstones, for instance, required participation by approximately a dozen groups and agreement necessitated a level of abstraction that made orderly execution problematic. Consequently, implementation required the development of a separate Implementation Plan and Accountability Process that offered meaning and key indicators for moving forward on Cornerstones. These were viewed as guidelines, not mandates. As the chancellor and vice chancellor pointed out, they were often frustrated by the slow pace of change, but acknowledged that (1) each campus president had to determine how best to proceed locally, (2) faculty could not be compelled to support or participate during implementation, and (3) the process of high involvement through shared governance might be as important as the product. Based on this need to maintain system-individual campus equilibrium, campus alignment with Cornerstones and the Accountability Process was rarely discussed collectively at meetings of the presidents, although the chancellor and vice chancellor did use the accountability process to keep campus presidents focused on system priorities. Moreover, the presidents were increasingly incorporating the accountability indicators into their own campus plans and assessments. It became apparent to us, however, that this was the result of ongoing "jawboning" by the chancellor's office and that the overall success of Cornerstones was the cumulative success of each campus. Even within this framework, we were somewhat surprised to learn that many of our campus presidents were unaware of strategic planning activities on other campuses. From our perspective, this certainly limited learning in the premier learning setting.

While the campus presidents were paying increased attention to the goals and indicators from Cornerstones and the Accountability Process, several presidents forcefully noted that they had their own set of "pressing campus issues," some immediate, some strategic, that were their primary focus. For them, adoption of a campus strategic planning process became the umbrella for obtaining support for their agenda. Depending on the campus, for example, it represented the means to revise plans developed by their predecessors, solve seemingly intransigent problems, or rally support for a new, expansive vision. As we listened to the presidents in this study, it became clear that they were confident that they could lead as they chose. While they believed that the chancellor's office was a somewhat powerful constituency whose demands needed to be taken into account, they were absolutely positive that the academic milieu insured their primacy.

At the campus level, the presidents, whether engaged in formal strategic planning or not, were unanimously concerned with obtaining high involvement by their local constituencies, ranging from faculty to staff to students, from business to government to community-based organizations to donors. By using a technique such as the charette process and by endlessly communicating their visions, these presidents insured a very deliberate approach to reaching consensus and moving forward. Although the time required would have been inconceivable for either Hewlett-Packard or Los Angeles County, it appeared quite adequate for academic institutions. Moreover, since the presidents controlled their local budgets, they were able to "walk the walk" by allocating resources to the outcomes. In general, we saw these presidents as the "poster children" for the saying, "slow and steady wins the race."

A Note on Differences

Throughout the book, we have highlighted the similarities between the three organizations studied, focusing on both the environmental forces affecting each and the tensions that can result from balancing centralized control with the need for local autonomy. From a leader's perspective, however, important differences exist between the three, which an executive switching jobs would quickly observe. For example, H-P primarily exists to improve shareholder return; Los Angeles County and the California State University seek to serve the public. While H-P's business units are becoming highly interdependent and the County's departments are moving toward greater linkages,

the CSU campuses are geographic islands committed to campus indepen-
dence. Moreover, the laborious, "slow and steady" approach to strategic formulation and execution so necessary in the CSU would seem foreign and
potentially deadly at fast-paced H-P and vice versa. Therefore, while all three
organizations experience somewhat similar external environments, we must
not overlook the fact that they represent three distinct entities that use different strategies to adapt and prosper within their unique niches.

Closing Thoughts II

As these leaders described the merits and drawbacks of strategy formulation
and execution within their respective organizations, we again found ourselves
mulling over several ideas implicit in their comments. We discuss three additional explorations.

First, since the early 1990s, it has become commonplace for observers of
the strategic planning field to assume that a major reframing has been occurring in the strategy formulation process. Simply stated, it has been argued
that based on the demands of a increasingly turbulent environment, as described in chapter 1, organizations have sought to accelerate strategy making, to increase their capacity for faster and more flexible responses to changes
in their environment.[2] It seemed to us that speed in strategy formulation and
subsequent execution would be an imperative for Hewlett-Packard, which
operated in a highly uncertain, very competitive environment, and somewhat
important to Los Angeles County, which was experiencing the greatest turbulence, but could take comfort in the simple fact that there were few viable
alternatives for government provided services.

As initially discussed by many of the leaders in this study, all three organizations were committed to a deliberate strategic planning process at the
highest level (i.e., conducting an environmental scan; identifying strategic
issues and goals; developing strategies, metrics, and action plans). Moreover, in both the County and the CSU this controlled approach cascaded
down to the County departments and campuses respectively—very formal
strategic planning existed nearly everywhere. Several operational leaders gave
the impression that these formal plans were truly appreciated, since they (1)
provided insight into executive leadership thinking, (2) offered a road map
for aligning local purposes and goals, and (3) set clear metrics for success.
Within this formal framework, however, we also discovered the threads of a
more agile strategy formulation process. That is, regardless of sector, we
found that the leaders at the operational level had a clear strategic intent for
their organizational unit and took actions to fulfill their vision. Many of these
leaders expressed their willingness to adjust their actions to make their intent

happen. Indeed, in all three organizations, the terms "flexible" and "change-able" seemed embedded among operational leaders when describing strat-egy in a day-to-day world. Several, in each sector, even used the word "improvise" to describe how they managed the strategy-making and execu-tion process over a period of time, lending support to the idea that strategy-making at the operational level resembles a jazz band, improvising as it progresses—the intent is clear and alignment is necessary, but the specific means to the end may vary.

For us, we wondered what practices might be needed to establish a more flexible and changeable approach to strategy formulation and execution pro-cess. From our assessment, implicit in the comments of several leaders, was the importance of "continuous conversation" as a best practice throughout the strategic planning process. As we learned from several leaders in this study, one method for enhancing their strategic thinking ability was to engage in "nonstop conversations," in which all discussions incorporated references to the external environment. These conversations provided a broader interpretive structure for decision-making. At Hewlett-Packard, for instance, unit leaders were encouraged to establish horizontal connections and program manage-ment to broaden their perspective and to use the new learning to explore pos-sible individual and/or joint actions; at the County, the Guiding Coalition and the scheduled strategic planning conferences became the arenas where any strategic question, whether formulation or execution, could be fully explored and "fighting for consensus" was the norm; and at the campus level of the CSU, presidents most valued their everyday interactions with both internal and external constituencies. At both H-P and the County, an additional perspective on the environment was obtained by spending more and more time with cus-tomers or clients. From our perspective, these continuous conversations were a form of action learning where leaders collaboratively shared knowledge of the environment to expand their ability to process, analyze, and evaluate informa-tion and then take decisive action. Done rapidly enough, continuous conversa-tion—as a form of action learning—provides an opportunity for ongoing self-correction, even allowing for innovative departures from the initially pro-posed strategic intent. We must note that continuous conversation can more easily be formalized within both the County and the CSU than at H-P, where the environment moves so quickly that each discussion could potentially refer-ence a different set of factors and, therefore, formalization of conversations would be a luxury and a very complex, dynamic endeavor.

At Hewlett-Packard, a few operational leaders advocated scenario thinking and development as a more formal practice for staying attuned to changes in the environment, thereby increasing their capacity for accelerated strategic decision-making. From personal experience, they suggested that the exercise of building alternative scenarios forced them to uncover key environmental factors and then challenged their assumptions and beliefs about the impact of these factors. Although the up-front work was very difficult (particularly the collection of data and information), they argued that it helped them determine which scenarios might hold the most promise for realizing their intended outcome. Also, by monitoring the environment and continually updating their information, they increased the probability of recognizing the need to adopt different means. Some of these operational leaders expressed disappointment that, due to cost savings, they lacked the needed staffing for monitoring, updating, and conducting impact analysis of changes in the environment. Although not mentioned specifically by the leaders from the County or the CSU, many of them offered scenarios when describing the forces in their environment.

For us, scenario thinking and development, as described, appeared to be another form of action learning and a method to share information and insight with those involved in the development of the central strategic plan. That is, the use of alternative data could serve as a linkage between operational and executive leaders to explore the myriad of possibilities, and also prepare the executive group to respond faster. This raised a most important question: Could the deliberate process of strategy formulation described in all three organizations accommodate regular infusions of new information? We believe not, unless the cycle time of the centralized, deliberate strategic planning process could be decreased. Although we did not hear about any efforts to speed up the deliberate process, this seemed to offer another approach to improving strategy formulation and execution in turbulent times.

Second, it became apparent to us that attempts to develop more flexible approaches need to take place at multiple levels. At the individual level, leaders must develop strategic thinking as an ongoing mentality by incorporating environmental scanning into daily activities—much like checking the weather each morning before preparing for the day. In this way, environmental scanning becomes habitual and second nature, rather than an explicit, periodic, and event-driven occurrence. As one CSU president explained, he makes environmental scanning the first item on his agenda at weekly meetings with his staff. We also speculated that by practicing daily scanning, leaders would become more resilient to the environmental shocks, as often described during the interviews and, therefore, more capable of timely responses.

We also concluded that the more turbulent the environment, the more complex the adaptive task becomes and the more strategy formulation and execution demand a group effort. As we heard from many leaders, due to the amount of time it takes to complete a situational analysis using the current controlled, deliberate process of strategy formulation, as practiced in all three organizations, the findings are often outdated by the time the analysis is complete. For this reason it becomes advantageous to speed up the individual steps (such as data collection and analysis, alternative generation, decision-making) through the application of group processes—areas that have been largely overlooked by the strategy literature and in strategy courses. Such acceleration might be accomplished by a "collateral" organization such as the Guiding Coalition, whose job is to assist and ideally institutionalize strategic the acceleration capability within the organization.

Strategy acceleration may also take place at the organizational level. Leaders need to touch base with peers or colleagues from different departments, as well as partner organizations, client and customer groups, and stakeholders. The more "eyes on the horizon" the better, as long as those viewing the horizon share information and insights openly. As one H-P executive stated, he checks in with his peers to "share weather reports" about the industry so that they all have a chance to stay closer to the "eye of the hurricane" and therefore the opportunity to see patterns earlier and respond faster.

Third, like most grounded research, this study uncovered ideas and concepts that we had not planned for—and which, we believe, deserve future research. We observed a surprising amount of variation in leaders' relationships with their environments, which we picked up in nonverbal behavior as much as through words. For example, some appeared to lament environmental turbulence, viewing it as an oppressive burden that was pushing them toward the breaking point. Others simply accepted it, viewing it as inevitable. A few embraced turbulence wholeheartedly, viewing it as an opportunity for growth. Are these variations due to differences in personality, background experience, or other hidden factors?

We also acknowledge that strategy acceleration has its limits, or point of diminishing return. We imagine that if the cycle time becomes too short, what could be thought of as "churn" would set in, whereby so much time would be devoted to gathering data from the environment that no plans would ever be implemented. Taken to the extreme, this could produce a state of organizational "attention deficit disorder," making it impossible to focus on any one environmental trend long enough to respond to it. These states would likely not be healthy for organizations or employees. But what are these limits? How can the optimal balance between stability and forward movement be reached?

Last, we believe that the term "turbulence" deserves additional research. As we learned in this study, turbulence can mean different things to different people. For instance, some may use it to describe an environment where forces move very quickly, while others use it to describe a state of unpredictability. Still others mean both when they use the term. What is the proper meaning? Is there a difference between speed and unpredictability, in terms of their impact on individuals and organizations' ability to adapt?

Epilogue

As we completed the final chapter of the book, we found ourselves reminiscing about the early stages of the study, some of the unexpected and extraordinary interviews, and the main organizational events that occurred during the intervening 18 months. We realized that the latter should be highlighted to provide closure for the reader. Below, we provide a brief summary.

Hewlett-Packard

- Although the merger with Compaq Computer occurred before the interviews commenced, H-P was in the midst of the arduous integration of the two companies, and this situation was uppermost in many interviewees' minds and subsequent statements. After the interviews were concluded, the Merger Integration Office morphed into the Strategic Change Office with a charter to facilitate the company's massive change management efforts. Most notable was the restructuring of the company to reinforce centralization and realign functional resources to better serve the three Global Business Units. This design intended to increase operational efficiency and effectiveness was unique for H-P, which customarily focused on growth strategies; it clearly reflected the slow pace of economic recovery and the ongoing sluggishness of the technology market.
- Consistent with the focus on internal operations, some initial downsizing occurred, targeting approximately 20,000 employees. Ongoing fear of layoffs during 2003 resulted in several external articles spotlighting low morale and the lack of management credibility. This resulted in stepped up efforts to solicit employee opinions and to communicate more frequently regarding the company's plans.

- H-P continued to emphasize the importance of anticipating the customer by (1) releasing 100 consumer products designed to work "radically simple and better together"—labeled The Big Bang; (2) putting forward an Adaptive Enterprise Initiative intended to synchronize IT and business needs in order to capitalize on business changes; and (3) sponsoring a worldwide initiative for the small- to medium-sized business market. Throughout 2003 and early 2004, H-P met most of its sales and revenue targets, but some margins were lower and the stock price declined, trading at a large discount compared to competitors.
- Although leadership shifts in multinational, complex corporations are not uncommon, H-P had experienced fewer substantive changes historically than other high-tech firms. After the Compaq merger, however, leadership changes increased, creating some internal confusion. Six months after the merger occurred, Michael D. Capellas, former Compaq CEO and H-P president for six months, left to become CEO at MCI. To H-P employees this was a disappointment, as he was viewed as a keen operational leader, whose knowledge and skills were much needed during the integration period. At the one-year mark after the merger, there was another exodus of senior leaders taking executive positions at companies such as Symantec, Adobe, Computer Associates, and AMD. Also, nine of the thirteen interviewed executives, as well as one of four strategy focus group members, left Hewlett-Packard.
- On February 9, 2005, Carly Fiorina, chairman and chief executive officer, resigned. While no specific reason was stated, speculation ranged from the inability to (1) develop a clear strategy in a complex marker, (2) please multiple markets, (3) change as quickly as the competition (i.e., IBM, Dell), and (4) develop acceptance of the Compaq acquisition. Also noted was the demise in the H-P culture and the poor morale throughout the company. To us, it appeared that H-P continues to struggle as it searches for an appropriate business model under increasingly turbulent conditions.

Los Angeles County

- The Guiding Coalition's maturation and accompanying assertiveness were the most significant occurrences, since the conclusion of the interviews. At the time of the study, the GC was tentative in its actions, testing its ability to force interdepartmental collaboration and uncertain about its relationship with the Board offices. During the next 18 months the GC made substantive progress on all strategic goals, providing confidence and resulting in (1) the establishment of many new cross-departmental teams, (2) the decision to define and operationalize the organizational values, (3) the inclusion of the next level of leadership at its strategic planning conferences, and (4) the expansion of its charter to take responsibility for developing initiatives to "enhance the County culture," plus the identification of strategic issues and the assignment and authorization of interdepartmental teams "to recommend and implement solutions." In late 2004 the GC undertook a major update to the strategic plan. Commenting on the result, many members noted its aggressiveness and the potential to truly change the way the County does business. Despite this progress, an underlying doubt existed. Privately, several members wondered if the process could be sustained if the CAO, David Janssen, retired during the next two years. Several members expected that it would take that time to fully move the GC from a collateral structure to a permanent entity. Given Janssen's long tenure and age, they feared that a new CAO could discontinue the GC. They still questioned the long-term support of the Board of Supervisors.

• At the time of the interviews, the GC had just authorized a pilot study in six departments of Performance Counts! (PC!), a performance measurement approach for assessing the effectiveness of County programs. Throughout the pilot study, the GC received feedback and discussed and debated new learning. Today, PC! has been extended to nearly all departments (and across departments when program outcomes require collaboration) and, importantly, initial efforts are under way to link program results and resource allocation decisions.

• The County continues to struggle financially due to the state's slow economic recovery and the ever increasing demand for services noted in the chapter. Moreover, the health crisis loomed even larger with the potential closing or reduction in services of a major County hospital in one of the poorest areas due to accreditation problems. Also, little progress has occurred in the introduction of new technology. On the positive side, a November 2004 amendment to the state constitution limited state seizure of County funds.

California State University

• At the CSU, demographics continued as a force. Tidal Wave II continued to rise, with projections that it would do so through 2011 before beginning to level off. Coupled with California's growth, this translated into increasing numbers of 12th graders graduating in California every year who aim to obtain a bachelor's degree. Racial and ethnic diversity also continued to grow in California, already the most diverse state in the nation, with the Latino population growing at a faster rate than Caucasian and other minority populations.

- The CSU continued feeling pressure to provide California, the seventh largest economy in the world, with creative, well-educated workers. Guaranteeing student access and instructional quality, however, remained a challenge due to fiscal constraints. The initial 2004–2005 California state budget released in January 2004 called for $297 million reductions at the CSU. Some relief arrived later in 2004 when a financial compact was reached between the CSU, the governor, and the California legislature. While not without controversy, the compact would guarantee the university's ability to plan for enrollment and maintaining quality—two tenets central to the CSU mission. The compact would restore $40 million to the CSU to increase enrollment in the 2004–2005 student year, and fully fund previous allocations made for student outreach, academic preparation, and educational opportunity programs. To raise additional revenues, CSU administrators made the decision to increase tuition fees by 14 percent for undergraduates, and 25 percent for graduate students.

- Technology continued its unprecedented impact, described by one top administrator as affecting the university more than anything since the invention of the printing press. With student demand for distance education continuing to rise, the CSU increased attempts to use technology to better meet students' needs. Increasing numbers of courses were taught using a fully "virtual" format, and even greater promise was anticipated by using a "mixed methodology" model that combines virtual techniques with periodic face-to-face learning. Sharing instructional materials via the Internet was also gaining in popularity among faculty, as was the use of distance-education technologies, especially among younger faculty who had used technology to complete their terminal degrees.

- The implementation of Cornerstones, now in its seventh year, was still on its 10-year schedule. Attention continued to focus on improving graduation rates, strengthening articulation with other colleges and universities to streamline student transfers, and doing less remedial education. In 2004, an Early Assessment Program was initiated to increase high school students' readiness for college and to reduce the need for remediation in English and mathematics of incoming CSU freshmen. Approximately 180,000 11th graders were tested in April 2004, and the results were fed back to high schools. The assessment program revealed that 50 percent of 11th graders met the math standards, but only 22 percent were prepared for English and writing, most likely due to California's rising immigrant population.

Notes

Notes to Chapter 1

1. While the concepts of Chaos and Complexity have gained credibility among social scientists, their practical application to day-to-day organizational life remains elusive; simply stated, they are too theoretical. As summarized by Marion (1999:5), "Many argue that Chaos Theory is a general theory of nonlinear dynamics and Complexity Theory is a subset of Chaos. Some would argue just the opposite, and yet others see little to distinguish the two. . . . To make matters even more confused, complexity has meaning within Chaos Theory." These theories emerged from the hard sciences and as social scientists, we recognize our limitations and choose not to enter the debate.

2. It can be argued that awareness of the formal, rational strategic planning process might not be appropriate in a fast-paced environment is not new. As early as the 1950s, for instance, Charles Lindblom, a Yale political economist, expressed skepticism about the benefits of rational planning, noting that in complex situations, decision-makers tended to engage in the science of "muddling through" (Lindblom, 1959). Lindblom suggested that decision-makers engage in a series of small steps and avoid making serious lasting commitments to a long-term outcome. In 1972, Cohen, March, and Olsen argued that most decision-making occurred under hectic, confused conditions, likening decision-making to a garbage can where decision-makers deposit different types of problems and solutions; successful outcomes were often achieved through chance alignment of these problems and solutions with decision-makers and available resources. As often suggested in today's discussions, it was not unusual for alignment to occur either after the opportunity to make a decision had passed or even before a critical issue became apparent. Similarly, in 1980, Quinn put forth a more purposeful version of "muddling through" known as "logical incrementalism," which cautioned against responding to radical, discontinuous changes in the environment using formal strategic planning. Quinn postulated that such responses would undoubtedly be made in haste and would likely be hazardous and irreversible; he suggested that managers make only broad, nonbinding, and reversible choices, so the organization can maintain more options and take time to gather additional information. Using this approach, strategy would eventually and intentionally evolve, albeit gradually.

3. It must be noted that some dispute the perspective that the environment is changing too rapidly for long-range strategy development. Michael Porter (1980), for instance, in a rebuttal to an article by Hammonds (2001:150), accepts that the last decade "has been bad for strategy," but blames companies for having adopted a flawed or a simplistic view of competition. He suggests that organizations have confused strategy making, which requires making choices and trade-offs that result in deliberately choosing a path to be different, with operational effectiveness, which should always be central to an organization's success.

4. The focus, therefore, is not on the testing of theory, but on building theory.

5. Existing relationships between the authors and individuals from each organization enabled access to senior-level managers and executives.

6. See www.qsr.com.au/.

7. Initial analysis of the interview transcripts produced over 30 forces identified by respondents. To be included in the findings, however, a force had to be mentioned by two or more individuals. A relatively low cutoff number was used because we reasoned that due to the diverse organizational units represented by the senior managers (e.g., R&D, corporate affairs; urban and rural campuses; human resources; fire department), their perception of critical environmental forces would naturally vary considerably.

Notes to Chapter 2

1. Corporate Strategy Board, "Stall Points—Barriers to Growth for the Large Corporate Enterprise," March 1998.

2. One could argue that the decision to acquire another company was a result of the external forces at play at the time of the investigation, namely, the economic, technology, and market maturity forces. Even if considered an effect of all the external driving forces, due to the magnitude and timing of the acquisition, it is included in this discussion.

Although this action by H-P was an acquisition, we noted three terms used somewhat interchangeably during the dialogues: merger, acquisition, and integration. The more colloquial use of the word "merger" was used purposefully by many to address this action as a "merger of equals," from whom similar and diverse capabilities, products, and services would be leveraged. Whereas postacquisition, the combining of the two companies was referred to as the period of integration.

3. This observation corresponds to a July 2003, International Data Corporation (IDC) survey of 999 North American business leaders who identified the economy as their most significant concern. *IDC Future Watch Report* 7, July 8, 2003.

4. Products that drive the early market move from the "early adopter" stage to the mass market "majority" stage and cross what Geoffrey Moore calls "the chasm." Geoffrey Moore, *Crossing the Chasm* (New York: HarperCollins, 1991), p. 21.

5. Gordon Moore, CEO at Intel, noted in 1965 and for the next seven years that every two years you can pack twice as many transistors on an integrated circuit— meaning every two years you get twice as much circuitry, running at two times the speed at the same price. Ray Kurzweil, *The Age of Spiritual Machines* (New York: Viking Press, 1999), p. 21.

6. hp.com, Major Events, 2/04.

7. H-P established a presence with a European marketing organization in Geneva

and the first non-U.S. manufacturing plant in Germany in 1959. David Packard, *The H-P Way—How Bill Hewlett & I Built Our Company* (New York: HarperCollins, 1995), p. 196.

8. Market events since the early 1990s, namely a mind-set of winning at any cost, damaged investor confidence and the public trust. This period of corporate scandals, involving Enron, WorldCom, Global Crossing, Tyco, and others, resulted in the passing of the Sarbanes-Oxley Act (August 2002), which was intended to improve quality of public disclosures on corporate finances and, hopefully, restore market confidence. Requirements for CEO and CFO (chief financial officer) certification on SEC (Securities and Exchange Commission) filings and other critical required actions indicate major changes for companies. Deloitte & Touche LLP Presentation on Sarbanes-Oxley Act, July 8, 2003.

9. Keith H. Hammonds, "The World Changes too Fast for Their Companies to Have a Long-term Strategy," *FastCompany*, 44 (March 2001), p. 150.

10. Packard, p. 32.

11. Packard, p. 81.

12. Packard, p. 76.

13. Packard, p. 80.

14. Interview with Jan Dekema, CEO, Stratiquest, Santa Cruz, CA; January 20, 2004.

15. Bill Saporito, "Hewlett-Packard Discovers Marketing," *Fortune*, vol. 110, no. 7 (October 1984), pp. 50–56.

16. John Young, "Business Planning for Competitive Advantage: The Ten-Step Approach," Hewlett-Packard White Paper, July 1990.

17. H-P Corporate Development, Ten-Step White Paper, December 1998, p. 2.

18. H-P Corporate Development, Ten-Step White Paper, December 1998, p. 2.

19. H-P Corporate Development, Ten-Step White Paper, December 1998, p. 2.

20. Interview with Jan Dekema, Stratiquest, August 2003.

21. H-P Corporate Development, Ten-Step White Paper, December 1998, p. 2.

22. Interview with Jan Dekema, Stratiquest, July 2004.

Notes to Chapter 3

1. California, Texas, New York, Florida, Illinois, Pennsylvania, Ohio, and Michigan.

2. NGO refers to nongovernmental organizations that provide public services (e.g., poverty agencies, health clinics) and may receive substantial government funding.

3. Adopted from John Kotter, *Leading Change* (Boston: Harvard Business School Press, 1996).

Notes to Chapter 4

1. California Postsecondary Education Commission; www.csulb.edu/~d49er/ archives/2002/spring/news/v9n62–tid.shtml.

2. In good years, when the economy is strong, the standard increase in the CSU budget is 10 to 12 percent per year to accommodate costs of inflation and enrollment growth of 3 to 4 percent per year.

3. The National Center for Public Policy and Higher Education is an independent, nonprofit organization that analyses policy issues in higher education. The re-

port card grades states' performances in five categories: preparation, participation, affordability, completion, and benefits.

4. The stated impetus for Cornerstones was, first, a desire to determine the CSU's future in light of a "crisis of resources" and a tremendous demand for university education in California. An additional objective was to optimize the provision of education in light of California's "continuing social, demographic, and economic transformation." The question was, in the words of the Cornerstones report, "How best do we educate our students for this new world?" (Cornerstones Report, see www.calstate.edu/Cornerstones/reports/implment.html, p. 2).

5. See www.calstate.edu/Cornerstones/reports/implment.html.

6. See www.calstate.edu/AcadAff/accountability/index.shtml.

Notes to Chapter 5

1. Somewhat surprisingly, our brief review of graduate programs in public administration and educational leadership found few descriptions that suggested strategy development, much less strategy implementation courses.

2. This is often described as a shift from a substantially deliberate process to an emergent process. The deliberate process is characterized by the step-by-step formulation of the strategic plan and a predetermined set of actions to realize the intended outcome. The emergent process is based on a set of decisions or a pattern of behavior that occurs "along the way" and collectively suggests intent.

References

Albano, C. (2002). How leaders think: The strategic mindset in leadership. http:/adaptive-leadership.com/indexb.htm. 1–4.

Association of Governing Boards of Universities and Colleges (1992). *Trustees and Troubled Times in Higher Education.* Washington, D.C.

Brand, M. (1994). The challenge to change: Reforming higher education. *Educational Record,* Fall: 7–13.

Brown, S. and Eisenhardt, K. (1997). The art of continuous change: Linking complexity theory and time-paced evolution in relentlessly shifting organizations. *Administrative Science Quarterly,* 42: 1–34.

Brown, S. and Eisenhardt, K. (1998). *Competing on the Edge: Strategy as Structured Chaos.* Boston: Harvard Business School Press.

Bryson, J. (2004). *Strategic Planning for Public and Nonprofit Organizations,* 3rd ed. San Francisco, Jossey-Bass.

Child, J. (1972). Organizational structure, environment, and performance: The role of strategic choice. *Sociology,* 6: 1–22.

Cohen, M., March, J., and Olsen, J. (1972). A garbage can model of organizational choice. *Administrative Science Quarterly,* 17: 1–25.

Collis, D. and Montgomery, C. (1995). Competing on resources: Strategy in the 1990's. *Harvard Business Review,* July–August: 118–128.

Cusumano, M. and Markides, C. (2001). *Strategic Thinking for the Next Economy.* New York: John Wiley and Sons.

Daft. R. (1995). *Organization Theory and Design,* 5th ed. Minneapolis/St. Paul: West Publishing.

Daft, R. (1998). *Organization Theory and Design.* Minneapolis: West Publishing.

D'Aveni, R. (1994). *Hypercompetition: Managing the Dynamics of Strategic Maneuvering.* New York: The Free Press.

Davis, S. and Meyer, C. (1999). *Blur: The Speed of Change in the Connected Economy.* Boston: Little, Brown & Company.

Day, G. (1999). *Market Drive Strategy: Processes for Creating Value.* New York: Free Press.

Dess, G. and Beard, D. (1984). Dimensions of organizational task environments. *Administrative Science Quarterly,* 29: 52–73.

Drucker, P. (1993). *Managing in Turbulent Times.* New York: Harper Business.

Duncan, R. (1972). Characteristics of organizational environment and perceived environmental uncertainty. *Administrative Science Quarterly*, 17: 313–327.

Eisenhardt, K. (1990). Speed and strategic choice: How managers accelerate decision making. *California Management Review*, Spring: 39–54.

Eisenhardt, K., Kahwajy, J., and Bourgeois III, L. (1997). Strategic decisions and all that jazz. *Business Strategy Review*, 8: 1–3.

Faulkner, D. and Campbell, A. (eds.) (2002). *Oxford Handbook of Strategy*, Vol. 1: *Competitive Strategy*. New York: Oxford University Press.

Glaser, B. and Strauss, A. (1967). *Discovery of Grounded Theory: Strategies for Qualitative Research*. New York: Aldine de Gruyter.

Glassman, A. and Winograd, M. (2004). Realities of public sector consultation: Information age challenges in government. In Buono, A. (ed.), *Creative Consulting: Innovative Perspectives on Management Consulting* (Research in Management Consulting Series). Greenwich, CT: Information Age Publishing, 325–344.

Gray, D. (1986). Uses and misuses of strategic planning. *Harvard Business Review*, November: 89–97.

Greiner, L., Bhambri, A., and Cummings, T. (2003). Searching for a strategy to teach strategy. *Learning & Education*, 2: 402–419.

Hamel, G. (1996). Strategy as revolution. *Harvard Business Review*, July–August: 69–82.

Hammonds, K. (2001). The world changes too fast for their companies to have a long-term strategy. *Fast Company*, March: 150.

Hatch, M. (1997). *Organization Theory: Modern, Symbolic and Postmodern Perspectives*. New York: Oxford University Press.

Hax, A. and Majluf, N. (1996). *The Strategy Concept and Process*. Upper Saddle River, NJ: Prentice Hall.

Hunger, D. and Wheelen, T. (2001). *Essentials of Strategic Management*, Upper Saddle River, NJ: Prentice Hall.

Jurkovich, R. (1974). A core typology of organizational environments. *Administrative Science Quarterly*, 19: 380–394.

Keller, G. (1997). Preface in Rowley, D., Lujan, H. and Dolence, M. (1997). *Strategic Change in Colleges and Universities*. San Francisco: Jossey-Bass.

Khatri, N. and Ng, A. (2000). The role of intuition in strategic decision making. *Human Relations*, January: 57–86.

Kiel, L. (1994). *Managing Chaos and Complexity in Government*. San Francisco: Jossey-Bass.

Lindblom, L. (1959). The science of muddling through. *Public Administration Review*, 19: 79–88.

Lissack, M. and Roos, J. (2000). *The Next Common Sense*. London: Nicholas Brealey Publishing.

Marion, R. (1999). *The Edge of Organization*. Thousand Oaks, CA: Sage Publications.

Mazmanian, D. (2004). Values and leadership in the 21st century. Working paper. School of Policy, Planning & Development, University of Southern California.

McCann, J. and Selsky, J. (1984). Hyperturbulence and the emergence of Type 5 environments. *Academy of Management Review*, 9: 460–70.

Meyer, C. (2001). The second generation of speed. *Harvard Business Review*, Reprint No. F0104B.

Miles, M. and Huberman, M. (1994). *Qualitative Data Analysis: An Expanded Sourcebook*. Thousand Oaks, CA: Sage Publications.

Miller, D. and Friesen, P. (1983). Strategy-making and environment: The third link. *Strategic Management Journal*, 4: 221–235.

Myer, C. and Davis, S. (1998). *Blur: The Speed of Change in the Connected Economy.* New York: Perseus Publishing.

Mintzberg, H. (1994a). The fall and rise of strategic planning. *Harvard Business Review*, January–February: 107–114.

Mintzberg, H. (1994b). *The Rise and Fall of Strategic Planning.* New York: The Free Press.

Mintzberg, H., Ahlstrand, B., and Lampel, J. (1998). *Strategy Safari*, New York: The Free Press.

Moorman, C. and Miner, A. (1998). Organizational improvisation and organizational memory. *Academy of Management Review*, 23: 698–723.

Nanus, B. and Dobbs, S. (1999). *Leaders Who Make a Difference.* San Francisco: Jossey-Bass.

Peters, B. and Savoie, D. (eds). (2001). *Government in the 21st Century: Revitalizing the Public Service.* Montreal: McGill-Queens University Press.

Pfeffer, J. and Sutton, R. (2000). *The Knowing-Doing Gap.* Boston: Harvard Business School Press.

Porter, M. (1980). *Competitive Strategy: Techniques for Analyzing Industries and Competitors.* New York: The Free Press.

Quinn, J. (1980). *Strategic Change: Logical Incrementalism.* Homewood, IL: Richard D. Irwin.

RAND (1996, 1997, 1998). *Report on Higher Education Policy.* Santa Monica, CA.

Ringland, G. (1998). *Scenario Planning: Managing for the Future.* Chichester, England: John Wiley & Sons.

Senge, P., Kleiner, A., Roberts, C., Ross, R., Roth, G., and Smith, B. (1999). *The Dance of Change: The Challenge of Sustaining Momentum in Learning Organizations.* New York: Doubleday.

Stacy, R. (1992). *Managing the Unknowable: Strategic Boundaries Between Order and Chaos in Organizations.* San Francisco: Jossey-Bass.

Stacy, R., Griffin, D., and Shaw, P. (2002). *Complexity and Management.* London: Routledge Publishing.

Sullivan, P. (1998). *Profiteering from Intellectual Capital: Extracting Value from Innovation.* New York: John Wiley & Sons.

Taylor, B., Meyerson, J. and Massy, W. (1993). *Strategic Indicators in Higher Education.* New York: Peterson Publishing.

Vaill, P. (1989). *Managing as a Performing Art.* San Francisco: Jossey-Bass.

Weick, K. (2000). Emergent change as a universal in organizations. In Beer, M. and Nohria, N. (eds.), *Breaking the Code of Change.* Boston: Harvard Business School Press.

Weick, K. (2001). *Making Sense of the Organization.* Malden, MA: Blackwell Publishing.

Wheatley, M. (1992). *Leadership and the New Science.* San Francisco: Berrett-Koehler.

Zemsky, R. (1995). Unpublished presentation at California State University, Northridge.

About the Authors

Alan M. Glassman is professor of management and director of the Center for Management and Organization Development at California State University, Northridge. He received his doctorate in labor relations with cognate areas in social psychology and organizational theory/behavior from the State University of New York at Buffalo. His research interests focus on the comparative assessments of strategic planning in the public and private sectors; the management of change; and the design of public-public partnerships. He has authored/coauthored four books and approximately 40 refereed articles; he has presented over 60 papers at professional conferences. Glassman has served as chair of the Managerial Consultation Division of the Academy of Management, president of the Western Academy of Management, editor of *Consultation: An International Journal*, and coeditor/editor of the *Journal of Management Inquiry*. He has been the recipient of several professional awards for innovative program design and contributions to the profession and has been an active consultant in both the public and private sectors in areas of (1) transformational and profound organization change, (2) strategic planning formulation and implementation, (3) leadership development, and (4) organizational assessments.

Deone Zell is associate professor of management in the College of Business and Economics at California State University, Northridge. Her research interests include organizational adaptation, strategic planning, and the diffusion of innovations. She specializes in the application of qualitative research methods to understanding phenomena underlying various types of organizational change. She is the author of *Changing by Design: Organizational Innovation at Hewlett-Packard* (1997) and the coauthor of *Awakening the Academy: A Time for New Leadership* (2002). She has published articles on

163

organizational change in *Organizational Dynamics*, the *Journal of Applied Behavioral Science*, the *Sloan Management Review*, and the *Journal of Management Inquiry*. She has consulted in both public- and private-sector organizations. She teaches courses in management, organization theory, organizational behavior and organizational change. She received her doctorate from UCLA in 1994.

Shari A. Duron has been a senior business strategy consultant at Hewlett-Packard and previously at Lockheed Corporation since 1986. She has also been an external consultant and managing partner for various boutique consulting groups, including The Graham Organization. She is an adjunct professor at Humboldt State University in the School of Business and Economics and teaches management courses. She specializes in consulting on strategy, scenario planning, organizational change, and leadership development in small- and medium-sized businesses as well as multinational corporations. She received her master's degree from UCLA in 1970 and her Ph.D. from Golden Gate University, San Francisco, in 1993.

Index